THE GREAT TEA ROOMS
OF BRITAIN

The Great Tea Rooms of Britain

Bruce Richardson

Photographs by
John Gentry

BENJAMIN PRESS

ISBN 1-889937-09-6

Printed in China

Benjamin Press
Division of Elmwood Inn
205 East Fourth Street
Perryville, KY 40468 USA
www.elmwoodinn.com

Other books by Bruce Richardson
A Year of Teas at the Elmwood Inn
A Tea For All Seasons

Acknowledgements

I recall boarding the Delta flight in Cincinnati, bound for Gatwick on the first of two pilgrimages into the world of British tea. Months of overseas phone calls, faxes and preparation had gone into preparing this expedition. John Gentry, my photographer, and I were loaded down with camera bodies, lenses and enough film for every conceivable situation. My briefcase was stuffed with magazine articles, guide books and recommendations on famous and not-so-famous tea rooms scattered throughout Britain. Topping it off, John and I were scheduled to have afternoon tea the next day at the opulent Dorchester Hotel with two of the best known authorities on the British tea industry.

It was at 35,000 feet that the doubts began to enter my mind. How pretentious for an American to prepare a book on British tea rooms! How would the tea shop owners accept our interrupting their daily routine? What kind of lighting would we encounter in some of these centuries-old buildings? Would there even be a market for a British tea book?

My fears were quickly relieved upon meeting Elayne Appleby, who oversees the elegant afternoon tea presentation at London's Dorchester Hotel. She and her gracious staff spent several hours assisting us in food setups and interviews. It was one of the highlights of our two tours. But that was just the beginning, as each tea room owner or manager welcomed us in, took precious hours away from their jobs to talk with us, and in many cases kept us well fed. We now have numerous friends in the British hospitality industry.

This project would not have been possible without the assistance of The British Tea Council and its executive director, Illtyd Lewis. The Tea Council feels strongly that the highest standards must apply to the great British tradition of "taking tea", and have founded the Guild of Tea Shops. Membership is by invitation only, and every effort has been made to ensure the highest standards in tea preparation. Most of the establishments in this book are members of the Guild.

I also received encouragement from Jane Pettigrew, tea editor of *Tea and Coffee Trade Journal*. Jane is a leading tea consultant, author and speaker on the subject of British tea history. In addition, she edits the Guild of Tea Shops directory, a handy pocket guide which no traveler in Great Britain should be without.

My thanks go to John Gentry for his wonderful photographs, his affable companionship, and for introducing me to the sport of darts.

Most of all my love and thanks go to my family for their patience in allowing me to be away to pursue this project.

THE GREAT TEA ROOMS OF BRITAIN

Introduction

A pilgrimage into today's gentle tradition of afternoon tea is a fascinating journey steeped in centuries of East-West trade, flavored with political intrigue, seasoned with high seas adventure, and now blended with diverse culinary traditions. Although the drinking of tea has been going on for centuries, the custom of afternoon tea has been around less than two hundred years in the western world. During that time it has developed into an artform which is now enjoying a remarkable renaissance.

It is sufficient to say that the tradition of tea is deeply married to British society. The average Englishman consumes three and one-half cups of tea per day. There is no more quintessential British image than that of a lady or gentleman lightly stirring a lump of sugar into a bone china cup filled with tea while a tray of crustless tea sandwiches and delicious pastries sits in waiting.

There is no record of tea being sold in Britain until 1657 when merchant Tom Garway offered it at his coffee house on Exchange Alley in London. While men spent their leisure time in coffee houses, ladies preferred the quiet, gentle setting of a parlor tea. Tradition has it that Anna, seventh duchess of Bedford, began the custom in the early nineteenth century by requesting her servant bring her a pot of tea, a few slivers of buttered bread, macaroons, cheesecakes, tarts, biscuits and small cakes to remedy the "sinking feeling" which she was experiencing in the late afternoon.

This "meal between meals" was taken in the privacy of her boudoir. She must have felt guilty eating alone, so she invited a few friends to join her. Those fortunate ladies, recognizing a fashionable trend in the making, soon were holding their own tea parties at home.

It did not take long for society to move the affair into fashionable hotels and coffee shops across the country. By the middle of the 18th century, tea had replaced ale as the most popular beverage of the masses. Outdoor tea gardens where whole families could enjoy this civilized custom—as opposed to the popular male-dominated coffee houses—sprang up in many towns. At the beginning of the 20th century, tangos and tea were partnered and tea dances were the rage of London.

Sadly, tea consumption dropped after World War II when many Britons discovered coffee again. Due to economic constraints, afternoon tea service now takes a back seat to the lunch and dinner trade at most restaurants. Only 53% feature tea on the menu at all!

Tea lovers are quick to recognize those shops and restaurants which take their tea service seriously. There is a certain smoothness to the presentation of the freshly-brewed pot. The accompanying scones, sandwiches and pastries are freshly prepared and displayed with an awareness of the visual presentation. The room is inviting and conducive to quiet conversation and the owner's dialogue with guests shows his/her appreciation for tea as a civilized artform. This is not always true in every situation, but there are those exceptional tea rooms and hotels where the importance of this custom is well looked after.

You will find the observance of this refined ritual gloriously carried on in a myriad of ways and in various settings—from fashionable London hotels and country houses to quaint village tea rooms. Some of these rural tea rooms served former lives as stables, cottages, carriage houses, or even Victorian milking parlors.

Can you imagine finding a 1903 tea room in Glasgow designed by modernist architect Charles Rennie Macintosh, which today is a mecca for students of both tea and architecture? Visitors from all over the world sometimes queue for up to an hour in order to gain a table in the Willow's Room de Luxe, located on one of the city's busiest shopping streets.

How would you like to spend a Sunday afternoon on a 20-acre London farm—complete with sheep, pheasants, a 300 pound pig and a peacock—enjoying a cream tea in an 1882 dairy parlor with walls of irreplaceable blue Minton tiles? Better yet, take a train across the Thames to Kew Gardens and enjoy afternoon tea in The Original Maids of Honour tea room. Tradition says that Henry VIII named his chef's small, round, sweet pastries "Maids of Honour" after Anne Boleyn. (This was prior to having her beheaded for not bearing him a son.) Not known for sharing his prize possessions, Henry kept the recipe under lock and key. Still, the owners of this 150-year-old family-owned shop will not divulge the secret formula for making their tea room's namesake.

Most tourists enjoy their afternoon tea at the same well-known landmarks. But how many travelers make the effort to drive nine miles outside of Bath in order to cross an ancient stone bridge and duck their heads through the tiny 300-year-old door of the Bridge Tea Rooms in Bradford-on-Avon? Rosy-cheeked waitresses in Victorian smocks wait to take your order, while Queen Victoria herself peers over your shoulder from the portrait hanging on the wall behind you.

Not all tea rooms are housed in sagging stone buildings or romantic thatched roof cottages. On pleasant days, you might want to explore the gently rolling Devon countryside until you come to the village of Tiverton. There, alongside the canal and its horse-drawn barges, you will find the Canal Tea Gardens–complete with a gigantic blue tea pot marking its walkway. (There can be no doubt as to the refreshment served at this establishment.) White-dressed ladies with smart blue ascots, fresh from the neighboring lawn bowling club, are often seated in the warm afternoon sunshine enjoying tea and sharing tidbits of gossip with one another. In the distance, cattle—from which your sinfully thick Devonshire Cream probably came—graze contentedly on the hillsides. Across the lane, a small boy leads a dappled horse which slowly plods along the canal bank pulling the Chinese red tea barge on its endless circuit around the town. In the downtown tourist area, an outstanding tea room with the eye-catching name of Four and Twenty Blackbirds attracts tea lovers from around the world.

If you love literature and the Bohemian lifestyle, there is no more romantic place to take your love on a sunny spring day than the Orchard Tea Gardens, located a short walk upriver from Cambridge. The tradition of taking a relaxed tea underneath the blossoms of the flowering fruit trees of the Orchard was begun in 1897, and it has been a gathering spot for Cambridge intellectuals and poets since it was discovered by Rupert Brooke, Bertrand Russell and Virginia Woolf soon after the turn of

the century. It remains to this day one of the very few places where, as in Brooke's day, one can chat for hours or just "sit day-long and watch the Cambridge sky."

Nearly every tea room in Britain serves tea as a sideline to its luncheon or dinner fare. The emphasis of this book is placed on the celebration of afternoon tea—sometimes elaborate, sometimes plain—but always in a fashion or setting that will leave a grateful memory in the mind of the celebrant.

—Bruce Richardson

THE GREAT TEA ROOMS OF BRITAIN

TABLE OF CONTENTS

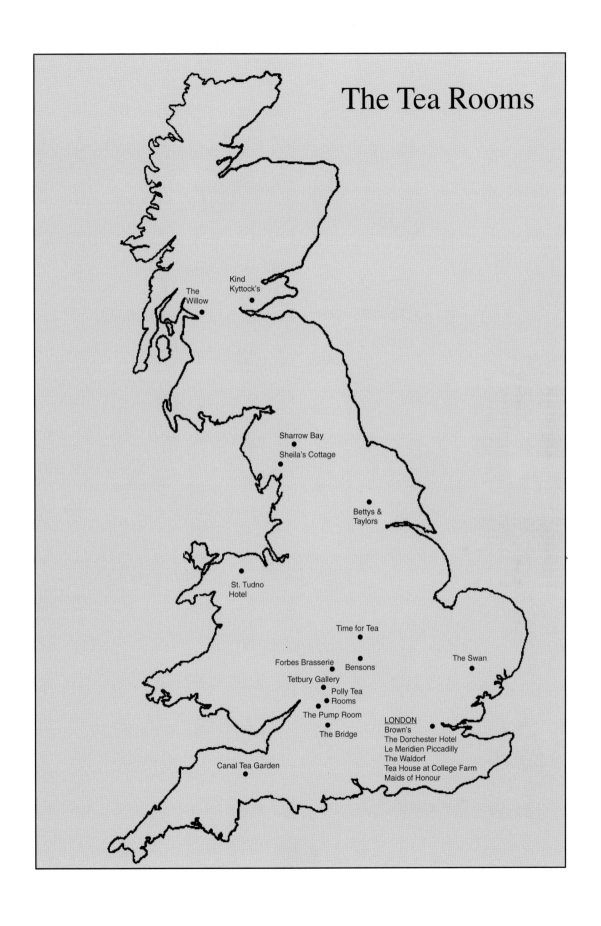

The Tea Rooms

Kind
Kyttock's

The
Willow

Sharrow Bay
Sheila's Cottage

Bettys &
Taylors

St. Tudno
Hotel

Time for Tea

The Swan

Forbes Brasserie
Bensons

Tetbury Gallery
Polly Tea
Rooms

The Pump Room

The Bridge

LONDON
Brown's
The Dorchester Hotel
Le Meridien Piccadilly
The Waldorf
Tea House at College Farm
Maids of Honour

Canal Tea Garden

BENSONS

Bard's Walk
Stratford-upon-Avon, Warwickshire

There is still much that William Shakespeare would recognize in his home town of Stratford-upon-Avon if he were to return. His house, the village church, and many medieval buildings would be familiar, but he would never have dreamed his birthplace would become a principal destination for tourists from around the world.

Today, crowds of school children fill the sidewalks, gift stores spill out their souvenirs at every corner, sunbathers fill the lawn along the placid River Avon, theatre-goers queue early for tickets at the Royal Shakespeare Theatre, and parking places can sometimes be hard to find. Yet, even with this fast-paced press of humanity, you would not want to miss out on a visit to the birthplace of the western world's best-known literary figure.

An early morning tour of the restored Shakespeare birthplace on Henley Street will help you avoid the peak crowds. Take a leisurely stroll along the river, past the theatre named for him, to Holy Trinity Church where he was buried in 1612. Make your way along Church Street to the Guild Hall, New Place, and Harvard House. Handsome half-timbered buildings along the way have survived for over four centuries. From there it is but a short distance to Rother Street with its endless collection of shops.

Be sure to visit Anne Hathaway's cottage in the town of Shottery. Located just one mile from Stratford, this romantic thatched cottage, set amidst a garden of wildflowers, is one of the most photographed houses in all of Britain.

A full day of walking and shopping will cause you to seek a quiet respite far from the madding crowd. Make your way through Bard's Walk, a restored indoor arcade of Victorian shops just around the corner from Shakespeare's birthplace. Before you know it, you will be standing before the skylit front window of Bensons Patisserie. A display of beautifully prepared pastries and gâteaux tempt your taste buds. You must enter and find out what other treasures lie in store for you.

A dozen small draped tables fill the

room. Original watercolors and live plants hang from the lemon-colored walls. Long loaves of French bread rise from the counter next to glass trays laden with fruit-filled tarts and decadent chocolate eclairs. Were it not for the Union Jack hanging from the ceiling, you would think you were in a French bistro. The owner, Max Lawrence, has worked in the food trade for years and he has a knack for knowing how the eye responds to a marvelous presentation.

A full selection of teas is served from a whimsical choice of colorful teapots, each decorated with a scene from a Shakespeare play. These pots are made in nearby Stoke-on-Trent and, of course, are available for purchase.

The full traditional afternoon tea begins with a selection of interesting finger sandwiches including: smoked salmon with cream cheese and strawberries; Blue Stilton with pear; prawns with melon and cinnamon; and turkey with brie and apple. Homemade scones with cream and strawberry jam follow. All this is but a prelude to the pastries you have been eyeing since first finding the front window. Lemon and blueberry tarts, mille feuille with fresh fruit, meringues, and Danish are just a few of the ever-changing pastries awaiting your approval. Mr. Lawrence's efficient young staff will make sure that your afternoon in Stratford is a memorable experience.

Unfortunately, Mr. Shakespeare died before tea was introduced to the British Isles. Had the drink found its way here a few years earlier, you can be sure he would have incorporated this late afternoon celebration into one of his scenes.

Lemon Tartelette

These bright yellow tarts are a sunny delight on even a rainy English afternoon. Bensons goes to the extra trouble of fluting the sides of the lemon before slicing the fruit ever-so-thin for the top decoration.

Pastry

1-3/4 cups	all purpose flour
5 ounces	butter, room temperature
1/4 cup	sugar
1	egg
pinch	salt

Sift the flour. Gently blend in the softened butter to a sandy texture. Make a well in the center of the mixture and add the sugar along with the beaten egg and salt. Work the mixture until a smooth dough is formed. Place in the refrigerator for 1 hour.

Preheat the oven to 350° F. Prepare a flan ring with a coating of butter. Roll out the dough and line the flan. Place a circle of parchment paper over the dough and fill with dried beans. Bake for 15 minutes. Remove beans.

Filling

4	lemons
9	eggs
1-3/4 cups	sugar
1-1/2 cups	heavy cream
	confectioners' sugar

Grate the zest from all 4 lemons and squeeze the juice into a bowl. In another bowl, break the eggs and add the sugar. Beat until smooth.

Pour the cream into the egg mixture and then slowly add the lemon juice and zest. Pour the mixture into the pastry shells and bake for 30 minutes. If the top of the tart becomes too brown, cover with tin foil while it continues to bake. Remove the tart from the oven and allow to cool. Before serving, dust the tart with confectioners' sugar and serve with fresh cream.

Bakewell Pudding

These delicious puddings, sometimes called "tarts," originated north of Stratford in the small Derbyshire village of Bakewell. This pudding is unusual in that an egg mixture is spread over the top of a straw-berry preserve-covered pastry before baking.

Pastry

1-3/4 cups	all purpose flour
5 ounces	butter, room temperature
1/4 cup	sugar
1	egg
pinch	salt

Sift the flour. Gently blend in the softened butter to a sandy texture. Make a well in the center of the mixture. Add the sugar, beaten egg, and salt. Work the mixture until a smooth dough is formed. Place in a refrigerator for 1 hour.

Filling

1/4 cup	strawberry preserves
4 ounces	butter
1/2 cup	sugar
4	eggs, beaten
2/3 cup	ground almonds

Preheat the oven to 400° F. Roll out the pastry and line a flan ring. Pierce the bottom of the crust with a fork. Spread with strawberry preserves.

Cream the butter and sugar together until light and fluffy. Stir in the beaten eggs and ground almonds. Pour this mixture over the jam. Bake for 30 minutes or until the filling is set. Allow the pudding to cool for 15 minutes before removing the flan ring. Slice and serve warm with custard or whipped cream.

Cotswold Broth

A hearty soup, such as this potato recipe from the Cotswolds, is a nice addition to a high tea on a chilly day. High tea is a meal served after 5:30 and should not be mistaken for the usually lighter afternoon tea served mid-afternoon.

1 pound	potatoes
1 pound	leeks
3 ounces	butter
2 cups	water
	salt and pepper to taste
pinch	fresh coriander
3/4 cup	milk

Peel the potatoes and cut into small chunks. Trim the leeks and cut into 1/2 inch lengths. Wash the leeks thoroughly and allow to drain.

Melt the butter in a large pan and then add the leeks. Cover and simmer on low heat until soft. Do not brown. Add the water and potatoes, increasing the heat slightly. Add salt, pepper, and coriander. Simmer for 30 minutes. Allow to cool slightly and then blend in a food processor.

Add the milk and return to heat for 5 to 10 minutes. Pour into bowls and top with sour cream and fresh parsley. A loaf of freshly baked wholegrain bread makes a nice accompaniment.

BETTYS & TAYLORS TEA ROOMS

Harrogate, York, Ilkley and Northallerton, Yorkshire

At the turn of the century, Frederick Belmont, a young Swiss confectioner, emigrated to England. Upon arrival in London, unable to speak a word of English, he boarded the wrong train and an hour later found himself in the dales of North Yorkshire. The air there seemed as clear and sweet as in his native Alps so he decided to stay and pursue his vocation. In 1919, he opened his first Café Tea Rooms in the fashionable spa town of Harrogate.

Belmont's natural Swiss flair for hospitality and his mouthwatering cakes soon brought him both royal patronage and popular acclaim. At a time when gentlemen's clubs flourished, Bettys Tea Rooms offered the ladies of Harrogate a safe place to meet and chat away their afternoons. Even a small orchestra was hired to accompany the afternoon teas.

The 20s and 30s saw Bettys Cafes opening in other popular Yorkshire towns—Ilkley, York, and Northallerton. As a brilliant confectioner Frederick Belmont baked all the cakes and bread for his cafes. His thriving business allowed him to build his own bakery in 1922 to meet the growing demand for Bettys products. Cakes, breads, scones, muffins, and chocolates are still made fresh daily at Bettys Bakery and delivered to their cafes as the morning sun rises.

In the 1960s, Bettys bought their own tea and coffee company from their friends and close rivals, the Taylor family. They added the charming Taylors Tea Room on historic Stonegate street in Old York to their collection. All of the shops carry a full line of outstanding teas sold under the Taylors name.

In Bettys kitchens, Belmont's principle of everything being "fresh and dainty" continues today. All dishes are prepared on the premises and are freshly cooked. Bettys Tea Rooms are now owned and managed by descendants of Frederick Belmont. The Swiss connection is still very much alive with their bakers and confectioners training at the famous Richemont College in Lucerne.

Tea lovers will appreciate the efficient staff and consistent quality found at each

Fat Rascals

These chubby scones from Yorkshire are a trade-mark of Bettys Tea Rooms. They originally came from the villages about the North Riding moors. The toothy creations are especially delightful for children.

1-3/4 cups	plain flour, sifted
1/2 teaspoon	baking powder
pinch	salt
4 ounces	butter, softened
1/3 cup	superfine sugar
1/4 cup	orange zest
1/3 cup	currants
1/4 cup	milk and water mixed
12	maraschino cherries
20	almond slices
2 tablespoons	sugar

location. You may enjoy a full afternoon tea or a simple cream tea. If you do not have long to linger, order Bettys' specialty—a warm, plump, fruity scone with spices, citrus peels, almonds and cherries called a "Fat Rascal."

A traditional Yorkshire afternoon tea at Bettys or Taylors includes a roast ham or breast of chicken sandwich, scones with whipped cream and strawberry preserves, and a Yorkshire curd tart.

The identity of Betty still remains a family secret, and although many tales are told and explanations offered, some mysteries are better left unsolved.

Yorkshire is a wonderland of small villages and rugged dales waiting to be discovered. This is the home of James Harriot and the setting for his *All Creatures Great and Small.* It is also the region where delicious Wensleydale cheese is made. Don't miss the opportunity to wander the mystical ruins of Bolten Abbey or travel down a portion of the 1,100 miles of walkways in the Yorkshire National Park.

Preheat the oven to 400° F. Grease a baking sheet. Mix together the flour, baking powder, and salt. Rub in the butter. Mix in the sugar, orange zest, and currants. Add enough milk and water to make the dough firm.

On a floured board, roll out the dough to 1/2-inch thickness and cut out circles using a 4 or 5-inch cutter. Place on the prepared sheet and lightly sprinkle with sugar. Make a face on the Fat Rascal by placing two maraschino cherries for the eyes and 3 sliced almonds for the teeth. Bake for 20 to 25 minutes or until golden. Remove from the oven and lift carefully onto a wire rack to cool. Makes 6.

Yule Loaf

No Yorkshire Christmas celebration is complete without a traditional Yule Loaf. You may serve it as a tea bread or toasted for a Christmas morning breakfast.

1 ounce	yeast
3/4 cup	milk (tepid)
1-1/2 tablespoons	superfine sugar
1/3 cup	plain flour

Preheat oven to 400° F. Dissolve the yeast in the milk, then place in a bowl with 1-1/2 tablespoons sugar and 1/3 cup flour. Mix together and leave to stand, covered, in a warm place until the top becomes frothy.

1-1/2 cup	plain flour
1 teaspoon	allspice
1/4 cup	sugar
1/4 cup	shortening
1 cup	currants
1 cup	sultanas or golden raisins
1/3 cup	raisins
1/4 cup	mixed citrus peel
1	fresh egg
pinch	salt
pinch	cinnamon

Place all the other ingredients in a separate bowl, then add the fermented yeast mixture. Mix well together until a soft, manageable dough is formed. Place the dough onto a floured surface and knead until dough becomes smooth and silky in texture. Divide into 2 equal pieces and mold into a loaf shape.

Place into two lightly greased 1-pound loaf tins and cover with a damp cloth. Leave in a warm place to rise.

When risen to the top of the tins, carefully place the loaves into a preheated oven and bake for 25 to 30 minutes or until the tops are a rich golden brown and the bottom of the loaf sounds hollow when tapped. Turn out and leave to cool on a wire rack. Serve sliced and spread with butter.

Sloe Gin Cake

Sloe gin is flavored with the tart, dark purple fruit of the hedgerow black thorn, called sloes. It blends well with the abundance of plums and dried fruits found in this recipe.

8 ounces	butter
1 cup	dark brown sugar
2 tablespoons	molasses
1 cup	flour
4	eggs
2 cups	sultanas or golden raisins
1-1/2 cups	raisins
1/4 cup	pitted, chopped glacé apricots
1/2 cup	pitted, chopped glacé plums
2/3 cup	mixed citrus peel
1 cup	sliced almonds
3/4 cup	red glacé cherries
1 teaspoon	mixed spice
	juice and rind of 1 lemon
	Brazil nuts
	walnuts
3 tablespoons	Sloe Gin

Preheat oven to 300° F. Place the butter, sugar, and molasses in a bowl and cream together. Do not over mix as this will make the texture too light and crumbly. Gradually add the eggs a little at a time, scraping down the bowl after each addition. Finally, slowly blend in the flour, prepared fruit, nuts, spice and lemon juice. Mix thoroughly.

This mixture fills one 8-inch square or 9-inch round cake tin. Place mixture into a well-greased tin lined with greaseproof paper and level off evenly. Decorate the top with the nuts. Bake in a preheated oven for 2-3/4 to 3 hours. Check after 2-1/2 hours. When the cake is cooled, prick the top with a skewer and pour 3 tablespoons of Sloe Gin over the top, so that it infuses the cake. Allow to stand for 24 hours before cutting.

Pikelets

Pikelets are baked on a griddle and are akin to crumpets which you find in the south of England. They should always be served warm or toasted.

3 cups	plain flour
1 teaspoon	salt
1-3/4 cup	warm water
1/4 ounce	yeast
3 tablespoons	warm water
1 tablespoon	baking powder
3 tablespoons	cold water

Sift the flour and salt together into a bowl and add 3 tablespoons of warm water. Whisk together until a smooth batter is achieved. Dissolve the yeast in 3 tablespoons of warm water, then add to the flour batter and whisk again until evenly distributed.

Leave the batter in the bowl and cover with a damp cloth or plastic bag for 1-1/2 hours. After this time has elapsed, the batter should look quite frothy and it will have risen up the bowl slightly. Now dissolve the baking powder in the cold water and add this to the flour batter and mix well. The batter should now be quite thin and runny. If it is still thick, add a little more liquid. Use the batter immediately.

Your griddle should be very lightly greased and hot. Drop a tablespoon of mixture onto the surface. As it spreads out it should start to set and as the bubbles appear they should burst and produce a holey texture. When the top is no longer tacky, flip the pikelet and brown the top lightly. This process is fairly quick, if the griddle is hot, taking 1 to 2 minutes. Serve pikelets toasted and spread with butter. Makes 20.

Earl Grey Cake

What could be more English than a cake flavored with the slightly citrus aroma of a good Earl Grey tea?

	Earl Grey Tea
1 cup	boiling water
1 cup	glacé cherries
1-3/4 cup	currants
1-3/4 cup	sultanas
1/2 cup	mixed peel
1/2 cup	butter
1/3 cup	margarine

1 cup	soft brown sugar
3	eggs, beaten
1-1/2 cups	plain flour, sifted
1/2 cup	ground almonds
1/2 cup	chopped walnuts
	walnut halves for decorating

Pour boiling water over a tea ball or tea bag of Earl Grey tea and allow to steep for 30 minutes. Remove the tea leaves and reserve the liquid. Place all the dried fruits into a bowl and pour in the tea. Allow to soak overnight.

Preheat the oven to 300° F. Place the butter, margarine and sugar together into a bowl and cream until it becomes light and fluffy. Gradually add the beaten egg, a little at a time. Blend in the sifted flour, almonds, and chopped walnuts. Finally, add the tea-soaked fruit and any remaining liquid. Blend together.

Grease an 8-inch round cake tin and line the base and sides with greaseproof paper. Place the cake mixture into the tin and smooth down evenly. Decorate the top of the cake with walnut halves. Place in a preheated oven for 2 to 2-1/2 hours or until a skewer, when inserted into the center, comes out clean. Carefully turn the cake out on to a wire rack to cool.

Wholemeal Date Scones

The secret to perfect scones is to not overwork the dough. Also, be sure you do not twist the cutter when you cut out the dough as this tends to seal the edges.

2-1/2 cups	whole-wheat flour
pinch	salt
1-1/2 tablespoons	baking powder
1/3 cup	dried chopped dates
1/4 cup	sunflower oil
1	large egg
1 cup	milk

Preheat the oven to 425° F. Mix together the flour, salt, baking powder and chopped dates. In a separate bowl, combine the oil, egg and milk. Add the wet mixture to the dry ingredients and mix into a soft dough.

Knead lightly on a floured surface, then roll out the dough to approximately 1-inch thick. Cut the dough into 3-inch rounds. Place on a greased baking sheet and bake for 10 minutes until risen and golden brown. Serve warm or cool with butter or clotted cream and preserves. Makes 12 scones.

THE BRIDGE TEA ROOMS

Bridge Street
Bradford-on-Avon, Wiltshire

Tucked into the western corner of Wiltshire, the little town of Bradford-on-Avon straddles the Avon River on the southern edge of the Cotswold Hills, only 8 miles from Bath. Overlooked by sunny terraces of weavers' cottages and Georgian mansions built of Bath stone, this lovely old town has a colorful continental air with quaint streets and venerable flower-bedecked buildings. Antique and specialty shops spill out their wares onto the sloping sidewalks, beckoning the passing tourists to stop and linger a while. With a hilly aspect the whole town directs its gaze toward the meandering river. The broad ford across the Avon was replaced in medieval times by a sturdy stone bridge, complete with chapel for the use of pilgrims. The ancient bridge remains the natural focus of the town; two of its 13th century arches survive although the chapel was converted into a prison in the 17th century.

Just across the Town Bridge and to the left stands the 300-year-old stone building that now houses the Bridge Tea Rooms. Visitors duck their heads as they step through the tiny doorway into an authentic Victorian tea room, complete with bust of Queen Victoria herself. This busy retreat is a favorite hideaway for both locals and tourists. The cozy, low-ceiling shop serves guests on two levels, each decorated with 19th century antiques and memorabilia from a more genteel era.

Waitresses scurry up and down the creaking wooden staircase bearing pots of piping hot tea and trays of lovely pastries. Their costumes recall the early days of London's first tearooms when white frilly aprons were worn over black dresses, and white mob caps covered curls and topknots.

The center of attention for those sitting in the first floor dining room is a Victorian oak buffet laden with a dozen beautifully-prepared cakes and patisseries. Each exquisite creation is made daily on the premises by pastry chef Kevin Nye. Typical pastry choices might include chocolate roulade, meringue with strawberries, chocolate gateaux, pathivia made with almonds, fruit tarts, carrot cake, walnut cake, chocolate and coffee cake, or a lemon gâteau.

A full afternoon tea includes a wide choice of sandwiches including prawn mayonnaise, Stilton onion and tomato, and Welsh rarebit. A toasted buttered crumpet, scone with Devonshire clotted cream and preserves, and cake of your choice follow in order.

"The days that make us happy make us wise," wrote John Masefield. Reluctantly, the satisfied guest must finally leave the Bridge Tea Rooms–much happier and surely wiser with a head full of memories of an afternoon well spent.

Carrot, Banana and Walnut Cake

The unusual combination of ripe bananas and carrots makes this delicious cake wonderfully moist and full of flavor.

2 cups	carrots, grated
4	ripe bananas
1-3/4 cups	sugar
5	eggs
1 cup	walnut pieces
1-1/2 cups	sunflower oil
4 teaspoons	baking powder
3 cups	self rising flour

Preheat the oven to 300° F. Mix bananas, carrots and sugar until smooth. Add remaining ingredients and mix thoroughly. Pour into a prepared cake tin and bake for 50 to 60 minutes, or until firm to the touch. Allow to cool.

Topping

8 ounces	unsalted butter, room temperature
1 cup	confectioners' sugar
1/2 cup	walnut halves

Whisk together butter and sugar until light and fluffy. Spread on top of cake and decorate with walnut halves.

Ginger and Orange Cake

This gingerbread cake is given a fresh look and taste with the addition of a zesty orange topping.

1/2 cup	brown sugar
4 ounces	butter
4 ounces	corn syrup
1/4 cup	dark molasses
1 tablespoon	ginger
1 teaspoon	allspice
2	eggs
1/2 cup	milk
1-1/3 cup	self rising flour, sifted

Preheat the oven to 325° F. Grease and line a 6-inch springform cake tin. Heat sugar, butter, syrup, and molasses until sugar is dissolved. Add ginger and all spice. Allow to cool.

Beat the eggs with milk and gradually stir into the sugar mixture. Stir in the sifted flour. Mix well and pour into the prepared cake tin. Bake for 45 minutes or until firm to the touch. Cover cake and tin in foil and allow to cool.

Topping

4 ounces	butter, room temperature
1/2 cup	confectioners' sugar
	zest of one orange
1 cup	chopped Brazil nuts
1/2 cup	orange segments

Whisk butter and sugar until light and fluffy. Stir in grated rind and spoon over cake. Decorate with orange segments and Brazil nuts.

Soft Meringue Roulade

This elegant dessert immediately captures your attention as you view the generous pastries assembled on the oaken buffet in the Bridge Tea Rooms.

10	egg whites
1 cup	sugar
3 tablespoons	cornstarch
1 cup	shredded coconut

Line a 10x15-inch Swiss roll tin with greaseproof paper.

Preheat the oven to 300° F. Whisk egg whites at full speed in electric mixer. Add 1/3 of sugar. Gradually add remaining sugar and cornstarch until whites are firm.

Smooth the mixture into the tin and sprinkle with coconut. Bake 10 to 15 minutes or until top is golden brown and slightly risen. Leave to cool completely.

When cool, turn out onto a sheet of greaseproof paper, coconut side down.

Filling

2-1/2 cups	whipping cream
	vanilla
1 cup	confectioners' sugar
1 pint	fresh strawberries

Mix cream at high speed with 3 drops of vanilla. Slowly sift in sugar. Mix until thick.

Spread filling over the baked meringue. Scatter on sliced strawberries. Roll up into roulade. Chill. Slice to serve.

Brown's Hotel

Albemarle & Dover Streets
London

In 1837, the year Queen Victoria succeeded to the throne, James Brown, a retired gentleman's gentleman to the poet Lord Byron, opened a hotel in fashionable Mayfair just a few minutes away from Hyde Park. Over the years the hotel became renowned for comfort, elegance, and impeccable service. It was simply known as Brown's. Victoria herself often came to visit; Napoleon III stayed there following the Franco-Prussian war; Theodore Roosevelt married there; his nephew Franklin honeymooned there with his bride Eleanor.

The first impression upon stepping through the doors, just a block off bustling Piccadilly Street, is of a country house in the midst of London. Everywhere one looks there are fine English antiques from rosewood dressing tables and beautiful Victorian and Edwardian stained glass to the handsome inlaid desk on which Rudyard Kipling wrote during his many visits. Entering one of the low-lit drawing rooms, one almost expects to see the smoke from Winston Churchill's cigar trailing up from an overstuffed armchair beside the fireplace.

Alexander Graham Bell was a guest at Brown's when he came to London to demonstrate his latest invention, the telephone. As a matter of fact, the first successful call in Britain was made from the hotel in 1876.

Today the style that made Brown's famous is preserved not only in the magnificent furnishings, the richly paneled wood, the original molded ceilings and elaborate cornices, but in the uniquely English hospitality and service. It is this sense of continuity that is perhaps Brown's greatest charm.

It is that same rich sense of English tradition which beckons tea lovers from around the world to enter this gentle haven. Guests are seated at chintz-covered sofas and low tables in any of several drawing rooms and secluded alcoves off the lobby. Crisp linen tablecloths, pressed napkins, silver tableware, fine bone china cups, and fresh flowers lend an air of expectancy to the celebration which unfolds daily.

A simple braided menu lists a variety of loose teas, including Brown's *Afternoon*

Blend. Following the tea service, a selection of crustless tea sandwiches, scones, and assorted pastries arrive on a substantial three-tiered silver tray bearing the engraved Brown's insignia on the handle. Your tea pot is never allowed to cool as the attentive staff caters to your every need.

This is the type of setting where you could easily spend the entire afternoon catching up on light gossip with a friend or sharing the tales of your morning's adventures rambling through the side streets and shops surrounding nearby Piccadilly Circus. All the while, the next Agatha Christie might be writing a murder-mystery in the window seat behind you.

Cucumber Tea Sandwiches

There is an art to making the quintessential cucumber tea sandwich. You must make sure the cucumber slices are thin, well-drained, and held firmly together with a good creamed butter spread. This will insure that the sandwich stays together until completely eaten.

Butter Filling

1-1/2 cups	butter, room temperature
2 tablespoons	heavy cream
1/2 teaspoon	Dijon mustard
1 tablespoon	lemon juice
dash	salt
dash	white pepper

Mix all the ingredients together to make a smooth spread.

2	6-inch cucumbers
	salt
1 tablespoon	olive oil
1 tablespoon	lemon juice
1/2 teaspoon	sugar
	white pepper
	fresh white bread, sliced thin

Use a food processor to slice the cucumbers as thin as possible. Lightly salt the slices and allow them to drain in a colander with a heavy plate weighing them down for about 2 hours. This will remove the excess water.

Combine the cucumber slices with the oil, lemon juice, sugar and a light amount of white pepper. Spread the cucumber butter lightly over thin slices of bread. Place one layer of cucumbers between the two slices of bread. Trim the edges and cut into rounds, triangles or oblong sandwiches. You may make these a couple of hours ahead of time if you cover the completed sandwiches with a damp paper towel and store in a closed container in the refrigerator.

Victorian Poppyseed Cake

A classic poppyseed cake can be found at many elegant afternoon teas. It is best accompanied by a fine light tea.

3/4 cup	poppyseeds
1 cup	milk
1 cup	butter
1 cup	light brown sugar
3	eggs, separated
2 cups	wheat flour
1 teaspoon	baking powder

Preheat the oven to 350° F. Grease and line a round cake pan with greaseproof paper. Place the milk and poppyseeds in a saucepan and slowly bring to a boil. Cover and remove from heat. Soak for 25 minutes.

Cream the butter and sugar together with an electric mixer until fluffy. Beat in the egg yolks one at a time. Mix the baking powder with the flour and then fold into the butter mixture. Stir in the milk and poppyseeds.

Whisk the egg whites until stiff. Fold them into the batter. Pour the batter into the prepared pan and bake for 1-1/2 hours. Let the cake stand for 15 minutes and then turn out on a cooling rack.

Combine 1/2 cup of fresh lime juice with 1/3 cup confectioners' sugar over low heat until the sugar is dissolved. Spoon the sauce over the cake slices. Serves 12.

Yorkshire Curd Tarts

Originally made in the Dales from the fresh curds left over after making cheese, this delicious cheesecake can now be found in most of England. It may be served as individual tartlets or as a slice from a larger tart. The tartlets seem to work best for afternoon tea.

1/2 pound	rich shortcrust pastry
8 ounces	cheese curds
1/2 cup	sugar
2 ounces	currants
2	eggs, beaten
1/2 teaspoon	grated nutmeg

Preheat the oven to 350° F. Grease 16 to 18 tartlet tins. Roll out the dough, cut into circles, and line each tin. Mix the curds with the sugar, currants, and beaten eggs. Spoon this mixture into the pastry shells and sprinkle with nutmeg. Bake for 25 to 30 minutes or until set and golden. Remove from the oven and serve warm or cold with whipped cream.

Canal Tea Garden

Canal Hill
Tiverton, Devon

You leave the elegant hotel teas of London and tourist-filled streets of Bath and Stratford-on-Avon far behind when you enter the west country of Devon. Its two coastlines are dotted with rocky coves, sandy beaches, dramatic cliffs and serene fishing villages, while the inland is a patchwork of farms anchored to steep hillsides between picturesque market towns.

The market town of Tiverton lies in the heart of rural Devon, high above the junction of two rivers—the Lowman and the Exe (Tiverton means 'two ford town'). This once-prosperous wool town owes much to the wealthy textile merchants who endowed the town with most of its splendid buildings—St. Peter's Church, St. George's Church, various almshouses, and Blundell's School. The school, where Samuel Wesley was once headmaster, served as the opening scene for R.D. Blackmore's *Lorna Doone*.

In 1814 the Grand Western Canal was opened—in a brave attempt to link Tiverton directly with the coast. This system of canals was originally intended to join the Bristol Channel with the English Channel, but the coming of the railroad in 1840 put an end to the scheme before it could be completed.

Fortunately, the canal at Tiverton was restored in the 1960s. A short climb up Canal Hill leads to the Grand Western Canal Basin and country park where tranquil surroundings and wildlife can be enjoyed. A small boy leads a dappled horse which slowly plods along the canal bank pulling a Chinese tea barge on its endless circuit around the town. The scene is an artist's palette of deep sky blues and hillside greens reflected in the rippled surface of the curving canal.

There, alongside the canal and its horse-drawn barges, you will find the Canal Tea Garden–complete with a gigantic blue teapot marking its walkway. (There can be no doubt as to the refreshment served at this establishment.) White-dressed ladies with smart blue ascots, fresh from the neighboring lawn bowling club, are seated in the warm afternoon sunshine enjoying tea and sharing tidbits of gossip with one another. In the distance, cattle—from where your sinfully thick Devonshire

Cream probably came—graze contentedly on the hillsides.

Devonshire cream in this glorious outdoor setting is the reason for making your journey here. Dairymen in this part of England boast of the fact that their cows produce the milk with the highest percentage of butterfat. For them there is a significant difference between common clotted cream and real Devonshire Cream. This might be the reason why the residents of Devon proudly place their clotted cream on top of their strawberry preserve-covered scones rather than under the preserves as the rest of the country does.

Clotted cream is made with fresh cream which has been left, unrefrigerated, to separate from the milk. This cream is then slowly scalded over steam. As it cools, the pure cream rises to the top and thick yellow crust is skimmed off and cartoned. Thick as butter, it is served on scones, Devonshire splits, and other sweets.

The kitchen for the Canal Tea Garden is housed in the only thatched roof cottage in Tiverton. Built in the 16th century, Lime Kiln Cottage gets its name from the lime kiln ruins just across the car park. Its teapot-covered whitewashed wall serves as the perfect backdrop to this lovely setting for a real cream tea—Devonshire style.

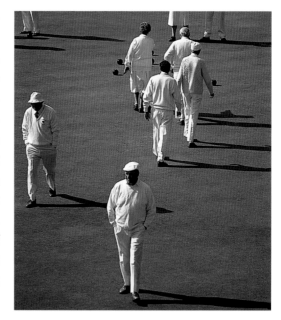

Devonshire Splits

This traditional cream delicacy is thought to have originated in Devon. It includes a filling of sinfully rich clotted cream and preserves. Splits are not likely to be found at an elegant hotel and are best eaten outdoors.

4-1/2 cups	bread flour
pinch	salt
2 teaspoons	active dry yeast
1 teaspoon	sugar
2 tablespoons	melted butter
1-1/4 cups	milk (tepid)

Sift the flour and salt into a mixing bowl. Warm the milk and stir in the sugar. Sprinkle the yeast on top. Leave in a warm place for 15 minutes. Mixture will become frothy. Use a wooden spoon to mix until a dough is formed. Turn the soft dough onto a floured board and knead for 8 minutes. Place the dough ball into a clean bowl, cover, and let stand until doubled.

Cut the dough into 12 even-sized pieces, knead each piece into a ball, flatten into a round about 1/2 inch thick and place on a lightly greased and warmed baking sheet. Cover with a cloth and let stand in a warm place about 20 minutes.

Bake at 425° F for 15 to 20 minutes. Remove from the oven and cool on a wire rack before splitting and spreading with clotted cream and strawberry jam.

34

Smoked Trout and Watercress Tea Sandwiches

Smoked trout, salmon, or turkey all work equally well with this delicious spread of watercress butter combined with a hearty whole grain bread.

2 bunches	crisp watercress
1 cup	butter, room temperature
pinch	salt
dash	pepper
1-1/2 cup	smoked trout
1 loaf	fresh granary bread, sliced

Wash, drain, and chop the fresh watercress. Mix it with the butter, salt, and pepper. Spread half the bread slices with the watercress butter. Place pieces of smoked trout on top the butter. Cover with a plain piece of bread. Trim crusts and cut sandwiches as desired.

Devon Flats

These flat cakes may be eaten with preserves and clotted cream or accompanied by orange marmalade.

1-2/3 cup	self rising flour, sifted
pinch	salt
2/3 cup	sugar
1/2 cup	double cream
1	egg, beaten
1 tablespoon	milk

Preheat oven to 425° F. Grease two baking trays. Mix together flour, salt and sugar. Add cream, beaten egg and enough milk to make a stiff dough. On a floured board, roll out the dough to a 3/8-inch thickness. Cut into 3-inch circles.

Place on prepared trays and bake for 8 to 10 minutes or until golden brown. Remove to a rack and allow to cool.

THE PUMP ROOM

Stall Street
Bath, Avon

The ancient city of Bath has drawn visitors to its healing waters since the Celts of Iron Age Britain worshipped their sun god around the bubbling hot springs which flow into the nearby Avon River. Invading Roman armies set up a military fort there in 43 AD and soon fine stone buildings and temples covered the therapeutic pools, the greatest in all of Western Europe. Although there have been continuous visitors to the springs for over 2,000 years, it was not until 1878 that the original Great Roman Bath was unearthed several feet below the city streets. This is the pool which modern day visitors explore.

A visit from Queen Anne gave Bath the reputation as a fashionable spa resort in the 18th century. Daniel Defoe described the fast growing city as "the resort of the sound as well as the sick, and a place that helps the indolent and the gay to commit that worst of all murders - to kill time." The town's stylish Georgian appearance was created by architect John Wood. His houses, public buildings, and gardens still dominate the city's character, making it one of the most magnificent areas in all of England.

Bath's heyday was long past when Jane Austen moved here with her parents at the beginning of the 19th century. Reverend Austen and his daughters resided in several buildings which are still standing today. Her days in Bath were still fresh in her mind when she wrote *Persuasion,* almost completely set in the city.

Resting elegantly at street level atop the ruins of the Roman baths is one of the most famous buildings in the city, The Pump Room. It was built in the late 18th century and reflects the prevailing classical taste of the Georgian period. Guests enter from the busy Abbey Church Yard, just steps away from the great wooden doors of Bath Abbey. This is the city's heart. Jesters, street musicians and tourists from around the world fill the courtyard throughout the day and into the evening as floodlights illuminate the great western facade of the church.

The Pump Room houses the spa water fountain where water is pumped up from the geothermal springs below. You may still "take the waters" there; however, the preferred drink today is hot tea for this is one of the best-known tea venues in all of Britain. Tea at the Pump Room is a gracious stop on a visitor's itinerary in Bath.

Gentle music from a string trio greets the ear as you step through the glass doorway opening into the magnificent tea room lit with fine crystal chandeliers. Smartly dressed servers work their way through the array of tables giving attention to every need of their guests. Tradition is alive and well here for this ritual has been carried out in similar fashion for decades.

As well as the traditional Pump Room Tea, there is the Champagne Tea with smoked salmon sandwiches, scones, cakes and pastries and champagne; the Tompion Tea (named after the imposing Tompion clock made by the famous clock maker Thomas Tompion) consists of finger sandwiches and scones; and the High Tea which includes cheddar and stilton crostinis and a selection of cakes and pastries. Should

you finish your tour of the baths by mid-morning and find your step a little slow, join your fellow tourists for *elevenses* which will carry you through the rest of your morning's adventures.

Bath is a wonderful city to see by foot. Walk along the riverside gardens and past the antique shops up to the Royal Crescent, or tour the Costume Museum and Bath Abbey. Less than two hours by train from London, this is a city you will return to again when you feel the need for a touch of 18th century elegance in your life.

Sally Lunns

Tradition has it that Bath buns were sold in the streets of Bath as early as 1727 by Sally Lunn, carrying her freshly baked wares to her waking customers. It was the custom to eat sliced "Sally Lunns" covered with scalded milk. Today they are sliced thin and buttered for afternoon tea.

4 tablespoons	butter
3/4 cup	milk
1 teaspoon	sugar
1 tablespoon	dry yeast
2	eggs, beaten
3 cups	bread flour
1 teaspoon	salt
2 tablespoons	confectioners' sugar mixed with 2 tablespoons water for glaze

Grease two 5-inch cake pans. In a saucepan, slowly melt the butter in the milk over a low heat. Add the sugar. Sprinkle with yeast and leave for 10 minutes in a warm place. Beat in the eggs.

Sift the flour and salt together into a large bowl, add the liquid, and mix well. Turn out onto a lightly floured surface and knead for 10 minutes. Shape into 2 balls and place in the prepared pans. Allow the dough to rise in a warm undisturbed area for about 1 hour.

Preheat the oven to 450° F. Bake for 20 minutes or until golden brown. Turn out onto a wire rack and glaze while still warm. Slice and serve warm with butter. Serves 12.

Pump Room Sultana and Cherry Cake

Should you enter the Pump Room directly upon leaving the Roman Baths tour, an incredible assortment of cakes and pastries greet you as you step through the rear door. This wonderful Victorian tea cake is a delicious choice to satisfy your sweet tooth.

3/4 lb.	sultanas or golden raisins
1/4 lb.	glacé cherries
4 oz.	butter
1/2 cup	sugar
3	large eggs, beaten
1 cup	all-purpose flour
pinch	salt

Grease and line a 2 lb. loaf tin. Preheat oven to 325° F. Cream butter and sugar together. Gradually add the beaten eggs and flour. Leave a little flour to mix in with the fruit and cherries. Mix in the fruit and remaining flour. Bake for 90 to 100 minutes. Allow to cool in the pan.

Milburns' Bulging Chocolate Muffins

Catering at the Pump Room is provided by Milburns, a traditional British company founded in 1907. They take enormous pride in their tea presentation. This delicious double chocolate recipe comes from their collection.

3/4 cup	milk
2	eggs
1/3 cup	sunflower oil
1 cup	all-purpose flour
2 tablespoons	cocoa
pinch	salt
1 tablespoon	baking powder
1/2 cup	semolina
1/4 cup	sugar
5 ounces	plain chocolate, cut into large chunks

Preheat oven to 400° F. Whisk together the milk, eggs and oil. Sift the flour, cocoa, salt and baking powder into a separate bowl. In the second bowl, stir in semolina, sugar and chocolate. Combine thoroughly, then make a well in the center. Pour in the liquid a little at a time, stirring gently between each addition until well mixed. Do not beat.

Put 12 paper muffin liners in a deep muffin tin and, using 2 teaspoons, divide the mixture between the cups. Bake for about 20 minutes or until well risen. Transfer to a wire rack and cool for 10 to 15 minutes. Serve warm.

THE DORCHESTER HOTEL

Park Lane
London

The reputation of The Dorchester among the great hotels of the world is unique in having established itself within a few months after the Hotel's opening in 1931. Ever since, The Dorchester's combination of elegant luxury, Hyde Park location, sumptuous decor and unrivaled standards of personal service has made it more than a constant venue for the famous and influential. General Eisenhower set up headquarters there in 1944. Somerset Maugham, Sir Ralph Richardson, Elizabeth Taylor, Alfred Hitchcock, Michael Jackson, and Barbra Streisand have all been devoted clientele over the years. A recent 100 million dollar renovation has now restored the grand hotel's traditional opulence.

Afternoon Tea at the renowned Dorchester is a grand ceremony which offers all you would expect from a fine English tea—sweet flavors, savory tastes, theatre, tradition, relaxation, elegance, and pure luxury. The palatial Promenade is the setting for this production which unfolds in the late afternoon, seven days a week. Guests are seated throughout the lengthy hall on comfortable sofas, facing low tables set with starched linens, fine china, and handsome silver. One's attention is drawn to the graceful marble Corinthian columns, gleaming chandeliers, French tapestries, antique mirrors, and magnificent planters of flowers which surround you.

Tea is served by a courteous, well-trained staff attired in English long coats. Although the setting is very formal, guests are soon made to feel relaxed by the attentive personnel. "At the Dorchester, we never say 'no'," comments manager Elayne Appleby. Indeed, the staff is, in large part, what makes a visit to this grand hotel such a memorable experience. According to actor and frequent guest Charlton Heston, "The cooks and bakers, the clerks and porters, the maids and flower ladies, the bellmen ARE the hotel."

Each guest is offered a comprehensive selection of well-prepared teas, including the Dorchester Blend. The teas are all supplied by a shop owner in Soho who occasionally delivers special requests on demand for guests who require an unusual blend.

The full afternoon tea unfolds one course at a time. The waiter arrives first with a silver tray laden with neatly trimmed finger sandwiches–sliced cucumber, cream cheese, smoked salmon, and the sandwich of the day. Guests do not have to fill their plates on the first offering because the waiter will return again and again until the customer says "no more." Of course, no English tea is complete without scones with clotted cream and jam, which are the next to make an appearance. You must pace yourself for the savvy tea lover knows to save room for the what is yet to appear.

The arrival of the pastry tray is a sight not soon forgotten. The spectacle of row upon row of freshly-prepared patisseries is almost overwhelming. Selections might include light citrus orange yogurt triangles, miniature coffee eclairs, fruit and strawberry tarts, chocolate and banana truffles, almond tartlets, apple and cream slice, and the *piece de resistance*—white chocolate parcels wrapped around a dollop of amaretto cherry mousse and dusted with cocoa. It is a whimsical work of art!

You somehow lose track of time in this setting taken from a page of Agatha Christie long ago forgotten. The sight of a celebrity, the conversation at a nearby table in an unknown language, pampered service—you have entered a world which you never knew existed. You now know why this adventure usually lasts for up to two hours. You don't want this indulgence to end.

Almond Tartlets

Almond tartlets are a common occurrence on many afternoon tea trays. Sometimes they are confused with "Maids of Honour" whose recipe is a little more complex. Dorchester's executive chef, Willi Eisner, shares this recipe.

Sweet pastry

1	cup sugar
8 ounces	cold butter, cut into small cubes
1	egg
3 cups	plain flour

Mix together the sugar and butter until just bound together. Mix in one egg. Add flour. Do not overwork. Wrap in plastic and refrigerate for 1 hour.

Filling

1/2 cup	sugar
1/2 cup	butter, unsalted and at room temperature
2	eggs (lightly whisked)
3/4 cup	ground almonds
1/4 cup	plain flour
4 drops	almond extract
1/4 cup	red jam
12	almonds
1/4 cup	apricot jam (clear)

Preheat the oven to 350° F.

Whisk together the sugar and butter until light and fluffy. Gradually add 2 eggs. Gently add the almonds, flour and almond extract. Do not overmix otherwise the mixture will split. Roll out the pastry to 1/8-inch thickness. Cut out round shapes and line small pans (2-1/2 inch to 3-inch diameter). Put 1/2 teaspoon of red jam in each.

Spoon or pipe the filling on top of the jam. Place 1 almond on top as a garnish. Bake for 20 minutes or until cooked and golden brown.

Allow to cool and brush with boiled clear apricot jam. Makes 1 dozen tartlets.

Tea Scones

The word "scone", thought by many to be Scottish, is actually derived from the Dutch word "shoonbrot" or "beautiful bread".

3 cups	cake flour
3 teaspoons	baking powder
1/3 cup	butter
2	eggs
1/4 cup	sugar
3/4 cup	milk
2 tablespoons	milk for brushing the tops of the scones

Mix the flour, baking powder and butter together to form breadcrumbs. Add eggs and mix for 2 to 3 minutes. Dissolve sugar in milk and add the flour mix in a steady stream. Mix for 2 to 3 minutes. Do not overwork the dough.

Roll out the dough (2-inch thickness) and allow to relax for 2 minutes. Cut out the individual scones with a 2-inch circular cutter. Carefully brush the tops with milk and then allow scones to rest for 1 hour. Bake in a preheated oven at 300° F for 20 minutes. Makes 20 scones.

You may make scones ahead of time and freeze them unbaked on waxed paper in a container. Simply remove them from the freezer, brush with milk and bake a little longer than usual.

Chocolate Eclairs

Eclairs are not difficult to make if you have a pastry bag. These miniatures are small enough to be eaten gracefully at the most elegant occasion.

1 cup	water
1/2 cup	butter
1 cup	sifted all purpose flour
5	eggs

Preheat the oven to 375° F. Lightly grease a baking sheet.

In a small saucepan, combine the water and butter. Bring to a boil. Add the flour and stir in slowly until a smooth ball of dough is formed away from the sides of the pan. Pour the dough into a mixing bowl and use an electric mixer to beat in eggs, one at a time.

Put the dough into a pastry bag and pipe onto a prepared sheet in the form of 3-inch oblong eclairs. Beat the remaining egg and brush lightly over the dough.

Bake for 45 minutes or until firm and dry to the touch. Allow to cool and then slit with a sharp knife.

Custard filling

6	large egg yolks
1/2 cup	sugar
2 teaspoons	vanilla extract
1/2 cup	all purpose flour, sifted
2 cups	half and half
4 tablespoons	butter, room temperature

Cream the egg yolks and sugar until light and fluffy. Add the vanilla and gradually beat in the flour. Bring the half and half to a slow boil and gradually pour over the flour mixture while whisking slowly. Begin whisking quicker as the custard begins to become smooth.

Return the pan to low heat and, while whisking, allow the custard to boil. It should become thick but not stiff. Beat in the butter.

Allow the custard to cool. Cover with plastic wrap and refrigerate. When cold, pipe into eclairs.

Chocolate coating

3/4 cup	confectioners' sugar
1/4 cup	cocoa
	boiling water
2 drops	vanilla

Sift the sugar and cocoa together. Add spoonfuls of boiling water and beat until a spreadable icing is achieved. Stir in the vanilla. Spread the chocolate over the eclairs and let stand until the icing is firm.

FORBES BRASSERIE

Cotswold House
High Street, Chipping Campden

The idyllic Cotswold village of Chipping Campden has an allure which quietly draws the first-time visitor down its ancient narrow streets lined with centuries-old, wisteria-covered stone buildings, and along well-worn cobblestone alleys leading to hidden courtyards and well-kept gardens. Somehow, the modern age seems to have bypassed this town.

Just off the main road and up winding Church Street stands the famous "wool church" of St. James, rebuilt in 1612 and named for King James I by two wealthy wool merchants who lie entombed, alongside their wives, inside the church. The churchyard lies full of sleeping souls who, over the centuries, have witnessed an endless procession of local congregates making their way along the tree-lined stone path to this peaceful sanctuary. It was in the nearby parsonage that a previous vicar's wife penned the words to the carol "The Holly and the Ivy."

The vista around each new bend of the road seems more beautiful than the last until, finally, you arrive at the 17th century open air Market Hall where butter, cheese, and milk were once sold. Its graceful arches frame postcard perfect images of chimneyed roof lines, leaded glass windows, brightly-painted wooden doors, and fascinating shop signs beckoning the inquisitive traveler to enter in.

Accompanying this unspoiled blend of physical and spiritual delights are choruses of bleating sheep on the surrounding hillsides. This is the Cotswolds at its best.

A handful of outstanding overnight accommodations and restaurants, coupled with Campden's close proximity to other touring sites, makes this peaceful village a perfect base for touring the Northern Cotswolds.

Standing across the narrow main street from the Market Hall is the splendid Cotswold House, the town's leading hotel. Tea is served daily in Forbes Brasserie, one of two Cotswold House restaurants located on the ground floor of three small houses that date from 1650. This charming eatery was once voted the best all-day eating place in the United Kingdom by the *Good Food Guide*. The dining area has all the warmth of an English pub filled with oak furniture and old photos lining the walls. French doors lead onto a narrow, walled courtyard where couples sit under a winding willow, leisurely enjoying their cup of tea. Afternoons slow to a gentle pace here.

Taking tea at The Cotswold House can be a savory experience with the addition of a hearty ham or tomato and cucumber sandwich, tomato and basil soup, or the famed Cotswold Rarebit on granary toast. But what really catches the eye of any well-traveled tea lover is the display of cakes alongside the pastry basket. The selection of homemade cakes includes Madeira, gooey carrot, or an irresistible three-layer chocolate creation covered with chocolate icing. Strawberry tarts, saucer-size chocolate cookies, apricot Danish, and scones with Yorkshire cream and jam complete the offerings—all created fresh daily by the hotel's pastry chefs.

According to its devotees, the atmosphere, food presentation, and welcoming staff are reasons enough to make stopping here a regular habit.

Cotswold Rarebit

The argument continues as to whether this dish is called "rarebit" or "rabbit". The story goes that a poor Welshman's rabbit was only a piece of toast under cheese sauce. Someone must have pointed out that the dish was not rabbit but it was a rare bit. Thus, a new culinary name was coined.

10 ounces	light cheddar cheese, grated
1 tablespoon	Worcestershire sauce
1/2 tablespoon	dried mustard
1 ounce	butter, melted
dash	salt
dash	cayenne pepper
	whole grain bread,
	1/2-inch thick slices

In a saucepan, combine all the ingredients, except bread, over low heat until the cheese is melted. Toast the bread slices in a 250° F oven until golden brown. Place the toasted slices on a baking sheet or ovenproof dish and top with the cheese mixture. Cook under a broiler until golden brown. Garnish with parsley and serve while hot.

Chocolate and Sultana Fingers

Sultanas are found in abundance throughout British tea time recipes. The Victorians rarely ate fresh fruit and often preferred dried fruits such as raisins or currants. This is a deliciously sweet combination of raisins, chocolate, and tea biscuits.

4 ounces	butter
2 tablespoons	corn syrup
1/4 cup	sugar
1-1/2 tablespoons	cocoa
1/2 pound	rich tea biscuits (cookies), broken
3 ounces	sultanas or golden raisins
6 ounces	chocolate (sweet)

Melt together butter, syrup, sugar and cocoa. Add mixture to the broken cookies. Add raisins.

Pour mixture into a baking dish lined with wax paper. Melt the chocolate and pour over the top of the mixture. Allow to cool and cut into finger-shaped slices.

Lemon Drizzle Cake

The refreshing taste of lemon has long been a popular ingredient in tea time foods. This cake goes well with a light Darjeeling tea.

8 ounces	butter
1 cup	sugar
4	eggs
1-1/2 cups	plain flour
1 tablespoons	baking powder
2	lemons
1/2 cup	confectioners' sugar

Preheat oven to 350° F. Cream together butter and sugar. Add eggs. Add flour and baking powder. Grate the rind from the lemons and then squeeze the juice into a mixing bowl. Set aside the juice. Add the lemon rind to the egg mixture. Place mixture into a prepared 8-inch cake pan and bake for 40 to 50 minutes.

Sift the confectioners' sugar and add to the lemon juice. Pour over the cake as it comes out of the oven. Leave in pan until completely cool.

Apple Cake with Caramel Icing

Apple cake recipes are found all over the British Isles. This recipe is enhanced by the addition of sultanas and a sweet topping of caramel and walnuts.

1/2 cup	sultanas or golden raisins
1/2 cup	boiling water
3 ounces	butter
1/2 teaspoon	vanilla
1 cup	brown sugar
1	egg
1-1/2 cups	self-rising flour
1/2 teaspoon	ground cinnamon
1/2 teaspoon	soda
1	apple, grated

Preheat the oven to 350° F. Grease and line a 10-inch round cake tin. Place the sultanas in boiling water. Set aside to cool. Cream the butter and sugar together. Add vanilla and 1 beaten egg. Stir in the flour, cinnamon, soda, and sultana mixture. Add grated apple. Pour the mixture into a prepared tin and bake for 30 minutes.

Caramel icing

2 tablespoons	brown sugar
1 ounce	butter
1 tablespoon	milk
1 cup	confectioners' sugar
1/3 chopped	walnuts

Combine the sugar, butter, and milk in a saucepan. Stir constantly over low heat until smooth. Do not boil. Gradually stir in the confectioners' sugar. Spread icing onto cooled apple cake and sprinkle with chopped walnuts.

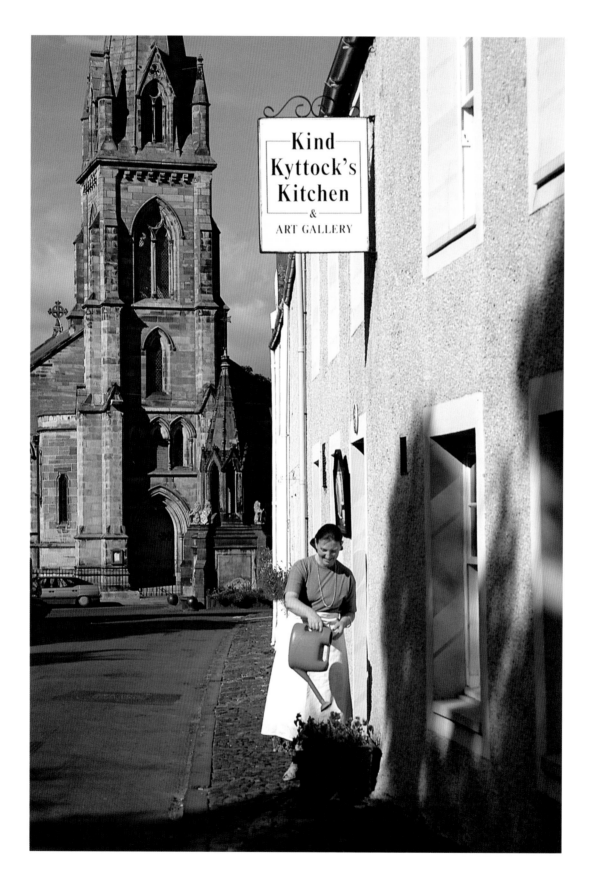

KIND KYTTOCK'S KITCHEN

Cross Wynd
Falkland Fife, Scotland

The discovery of an unforgettable village tucked away in the British countryside is sometimes the result of becoming lost. At other times, it involves the courage to leave the main highway in order to follow your instinct in search of the town that goes with the church spire you have eyed from a distance. The latter is the case as you travel the A91 along the Lomond Hills from Edinburgh on the way to the golf mecca of St. Andrews. To the right, the A912 becomes "the road less taken" as you wind your way a short distance through golden fields of hay, past centuries-old stone fences, and across a quiet country stream toward the wee village of Falkland.

Interesting, it is not the town church that first gains your attention as you turn toward town centre. To your right stands the magnificent Palace of Falkland, hunting lodge and retreat of the Stewart kings and queens. The medieval palace fell into ruin with the death of Mary, Queen of Scots, and was eventually restored by James V in the renaissance style. The first tennis court in Britain was built here in 1535 and is still used today; however, the tennis played by the Stewarts was quite different from that played 400 miles south at Wimbledon. The Falkland palace and its lovely gardens are now open for touring year round.

A short stroll up High Street, past antique shops and 17th century buildings adorned with fascinating marriage lintels, brings you to Mercat Cross—complete with a Church of Scotland and ancient village fountain. The street to your left, Cross Wynd, leads to your next serendipitous discovery, Kind Kyttock's Kitchen.

You are first intrigued by the name on the handsome red sign, complete with tea pot, beside the doorway. Why Kind Kyttock? Owner, Bert Dalrymple, will tell you that Miss Kyttock was the local heroine of a poem by William Dunbar, an early Scots poet. One of her virtues was serving good food and liquid refreshments to weary travelers. Bert and wife, Liz, moved here from Glasgow in 1970 to carry on that tradition of hospitality in their ever-popular tea room.

The aroma of freshly baked bread greets

you as you pass the kitchen door on the way to one of two dining rooms. Local sketches, prints of famous artwork, and china plates–all for sale–line the white-washed walls. A collection of Wemyss tea-pots fills the pine cupboards. In the winter, a crackling fire welcomes you out of the cold North Sea breeze. The soft tick of an antique wall clock adds to this relaxed atmosphere where community folk, and tourists from around the world, gather daily for refreshment and pleasant conversation.

The Dalrymple's homemade fare is traditionally Scottish. No one makes short-bread like the Scots. In this region the pie-shaped wedges are called Petticoat Tails, for they resemble the shape of the petticoat hoops worn in the 19th century. Other sweet treats include pancakes (dropped scones) with apricot preserves, Isle of Rhum gingerbread, traditional Cloutie Dumpling, Rob Roy Sweet, and cream-filled Braw wee meringues. It's hard to know which to try first. A variety of hearty sandwiches are available on homemade bread. (Don't look for dainty crustless tea sandwiches here.)

Following an afternoon in this pleasant setting, the refreshed traveler is ready to press on to neighboring St. Andrews, Dundee, or Perth. But for the moment, memories of sweet shortbread and a steaming hot tea mix with the storybook setting of this peaceful village. The less traveled road has led, once again, to another hidden treasure.

Drop Scones

Drop scones are known by many names such as Scotch pancakes or girdle scones. They are baked on a girdle, or griddle, and eaten while warm with preserves or honey.

2-1/2 cups	milk
3	eggs
5 cups	self-rising flour
1 cup	sugar
3 teaspoons	baking powder

Mix milk and eggs together, then add the other ingredients. Beat well. Let the mixture stand for 30 minutes. Depending on the brand of flour, more or less milk may be required.

Use a buttered paper towel to lightly grease a hot griddle. Drop the batter onto the hot griddle to make pancake-size scones, about 3 inches in diameter. Wait until the bubbles burst on the surface of the batter before turning.

Makes 26 scones.

Midlothian Oat Cakes

Oats are able to flourish in even the poorest of soils and thus have been a staple of Celtic fare for centuries. These baked oatcakes are more pliable and much easier to handle than traditional oatcakes. The original recipes called for lard. Today butter or margarine are suitable substitutes.

5 cups	medium oatmeal
1-3/4 cups	plain flour
6 ounces	butter or margarine
2 teaspoons	baking powder
pinch	salt
	water to mix

Preheat the oven to 300° F. Combine dry ingredients in a large mixing bowl. Melt the butter and add to the dry ingredients. Add enough water to make a stiff, but pliable, dough. Roll out on a well-floured surface and cut with a 2-1/2 inch cutter. Place the cakes on a baking sheet and bake for 30 minutes.

Allow the cakes to cool before serving with cheese or butter. Store in an airtight tin. Makes 40 oatcakes.

Petticoat Tails Shortbread

Shortbread recipes vary from baker to baker across Scotland. This traditional shortbread recipe takes its name from the shape of the petticoat hoops worn in the 19th century and originated in nearby Edinburgh.

1-3/4 cups	plain flour
1/2 cup	sugar
6 ounces	unsalted butter
2	7-inch round baking tins

Mix the flour and sugar together. Cut in the butter until it can be gathered together and kneaded into a ball.

Preheat the oven to 350° F. Press half of the mixture into a well-greased 7-inch round tin. Smooth the surface using the back of a dessert spoon. Using a fork, prick the surface and pattern the circumference to give a petticoat ruffle effect. Bake for 20 to 30 minutes until golden brown. Dust with sugar and cut into 8 wedges while still warm. Allow to cool in the tin.

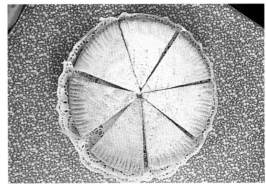

LE MERIDIEN PICCADILLY

Piccadilly
London

Le Meridien Piccadilly is a five star luxury hotel in the heart of London's West End. It is an oasis of restrained elegance and its location, just two blocks off Piccadilly Circus, makes it a perfect base for world-class shopping on Regent Street or visiting the theatre district, National Gallery or Buckingham Palace.

Le Meridien Piccadilly is, of course, everything you would expect of a premier hotel with an impressive lineage. Established in 1908 as *The Piccadilly*, the hotel was archetypal of high Edwardian style, becoming immediately famous for its lavish spending and subsequently enjoying the Royal patronage of George V. The hotel built a substantial reputation as one of London's finest hostelries, gracing London's society for nearly eighty years, practically unchanged.

In 1986 the hotel was conscientiously modernized, while retaining its Edwardian splendor, becoming Le Meridien Piccadilly. The influence of its French owners is found at the hotel today. Subtle Gaelic influences are combined with traditional British val-

ues to great effect. Nowhere is that influence more evident than in the grand Oak Room. Its four giant chandeliers and tall gilded mirrors remind you of the palace at Versailles.

This hospitable room, just off the main lobby, is warmed with the addition of wood paneled walls, comfortable wing chairs and soft couches set before low linen covered tables. Airy ferns in Chinese porcelain pots give the room a soft inviting appeal.

An interesting display of teas and Chinese tea bricks at the room's entrance allows novice tea drinkers an opportunity to view the various teas and tea blends before they are infused in boiling water. All of the teas presented are offered on the menu.

You may begin your afternoon tea experience in the Oak Room with a tall flute of champagne. After the tea is poured by the attentive staff, the first course arrives on a silver tray filled with a quartet of tea sandwiches. The offerings vary from time to time but you will always find such favorites as Scottish smoked salmon, egg mayonnaise and cress, cream cheese and chives with cucumber, or baked ham with whole grain mustard.

Scones with preserves and Devonshire clotted cream comprise the second course which soon segues into an enticing display of delicious French pastries– raspberry or strawberry tarts and miniature eclairs. A light tea is offered for those who prefer a less filling meal or just a pick-me-up which will carry you through an evening of the-atre and late night dining.

Tea at the Oak Room is a pleasant respite after a busy afternoon of shopping or museum hopping. Its elegant yet personable ambiance encourages pleasant conversation in peaceful surroundings—just what the weary tourist often needs in the middle of a busy afternoon.

Madeleines

These shell-shaped French sponge cakes are best eaten when still barely warm from the oven.

2	eggs, separated
1/2 cup	sugar
1 stick	unsalted butter, melted
	zest of 1 lemon
	juice of 1/2 lemon
1/2 cup	self-rising flour

Preheat oven to 375° F. Lightly grease 2 to 4 madeleine tins.

Beat the egg yolks and sugar until mixed. Add melted butter, lemon rind and juice. Beat until well combined. Sift the flour over this mixture and fold in. Beat the egg whites with a fork and add to batter.

Place a spoonful of batter into each mold, filling them about two-thirds full. Bake for 20 minutes. Allow to cool a few minutes in the tins before gently removing.

Makes 2 dozen.

Irish Lace Cookies

The texture of these elegant cookies will remind you of fine Irish lace. They may be made ahead of time and stored in an airtight container.

1 cup	unsalted butter
1/2 cup	all purpose flour
2 cups	firmly packed brown sugar
2 tablespoons	vanilla
1/4 cup	milk
2 cups	old-fashioned rolled oats

Preheat oven to 350° F. Grease and flour 2 baking sheets. Cream butter and sugar. Add vanilla; stir in flour, milk and rolled oats. Drop batter by the tablespoon onto prepared baking sheets; allow room for cookies to spread about 3 inches in diameter. Each baking sheet will hold about 6 cookies.

Bake 10 minutes or until cookies flatten and look dry. Cool for 4 to 5 minutes on baking sheets. Lift from baking sheet with a metal spatula and cool completely. Makes 4 dozen cookies.

Truffle Cups

Delicate chocolate cups serve as edible containers for an airy deep chocolate mousse. You may prefer to fill them with fresh strawberries or custard.

1/2 pound	semisweet chocolate– finely chopped, or semisweet chocolate chips

Melt chocolate in a double boiler or a bowl set over a pan of hot water. Stir until smooth.

Working quickly, use the back of a spoon or a small knife to spread chocolate on bottom and up sides of 6 to 8 paper cupcake liners. Set liners in a muffin pan. Chill until firm in freezer, 10 to 15 minutes, or in refrigerator 20 to 30 minutes. Carefully peel off the paper liners, handling chocolate as little as possible. Cups may be refrigerated for a couple of days. They will begin to turn gray after several days.

Mousse filling

2-2/3 cups	whipping cream
1-1/3 cups	confectioners' sugar, sifted
2/3 cup	Dutch-process cocoa, sifted
2 teaspoons	powdered instant coffee (not granules)
1-1/3 tablespoons	dark rum
	confectioners' sugar or cocoa– for decoration

Place cream, sugar, cocoa, instant coffee and rum in a large mixing bowl. Beat with electric mixer or whisk until cream forms soft peaks but is not stiff.

Spoon into small truffle cups and refrigerate until serving. Decorate tops with a dusting of confectioners' sugar or cocoa just before serving.

THE ORIGINAL MAIDS OF HONOUR

Kew Road
Kew Gardens, Surrey

An extended stay in London would not be complete without a stroll through the Royal Botanical Gardens at Kew. The 288 acres of gardens have beautiful walks, and the 25,000 varieties of plants are housed in a series of spectacular buildings, such as the Orangery, the Palm House, and various hot houses. The painter Gainesborough is buried nearby in the village churchyard. Several hours in this serene setting will make you forget the exhausting bustle of Central London traffic.

How do you top off an afternoon of viewing these world class gardens? With an equally memorable afternoon tea at one of Britain's most historic tea rooms—The Original Maids of Honour.

Those who are knowledgeable of afternoon tea fare are immediately intrigued by the name. The Maids of Honour tart has been part of the local history for nearly 300 years. Although there are numerous legends about their origin, it is generally believed that Henry VIII was the first to use the name after he saw Ann Boleyn and other "maids of honour" eating these tarts from silver dishes.

It would appear that King Henry VIII was so delighted with the desserts that the recipe was kept secret and locked in an iron box in Richmond Palace. Some stories go even further and claim that, in order to protect the secret, the unfortunate maid who invented the cake was imprisoned within the palace grounds and ordered to produce the pastries solely for the royal household.

By the early 18th century the recipe had been disclosed to a bakery in Richmond and the royal delicacies became one of the features of fashionable Richmond throughout that century and beyond.

The first Maids of Honour shop was opened in the early 18th century on the corner of Hill Street in Richmond, just down the road from the present site. It was there that Robert Newens served his apprenticeship and in 1850 opened his own bakery which continued the tradition of making Maids of Honour in Richmond. To this day it is still owned and run by the Newens family and they continue to serve their long standing specialty namesake

whose recipe remains a closely guarded family secret.

What seems to attract first time visitors today is the large bow front window which overflows with freshly baked cakes, cream horns and tarts. Devoted local clientele are often seen strapping a bakery box onto the carrier of their bicycles and pedaling away with the morning's breakfast.

It is the aroma of a busy bakery which first greets guests entering the shop. Mr. Newen and his bakers have been busy since the pre-dawn hours preparing their delicious goods for the day's appreciative customers.

Afternoon tea may be taken in the dining room at intimate antique wooden tables decorated with fresh roses and miniature carnations. A mixture of local villagers, London day-trippers, and respite-seeking tourists make up an eclectic mix of tea celebrants. It is a quiet room with a low ceiling, mainly lit with large open windows and an occasional lamp.

The set tea includes a pot of freshly brewed tea, two plain scones with clotted cream and jam, cream horns and Maids of Honour. The staff is happy to tell you more about the history of the shop and the neighborhood.

Kew Gardens is but a short 30 minute tube ride from London. Exit at the Kew Gardens Station and walk two blocks to Kew Gardens Road. The Maids of Honour is located directly across the street from the Cumberland Gate entrance to Kew Gardens.

Maids of Honour

The original recipe for this tart is still a family secret. This traditional English recipe is similar to the ones found in Richmond.

1/2 pound	rich shortcrust pastry
4 ounces	curd cheese
	or cottage cheese
3 ounces	butter, room temperature
2	eggs, beaten
2-1/2 ounces	brandy
1/2 cup	sugar
3 ounces	cold baked potato
1/4 cup	ground almonds
1/2 teaspoon	grated nutmeg
	grated rind of two lemons
3 tablespoons	lemon juice

Preheat the oven to 350° F. Grease 16 patty tins. Roll out the chilled pastry on a lightly floured board. Use a 3-inch cookie cutter to cut out the rounds of thin pastry. Line the tins with pastry.

Beat together the curd cheese and butter. Add the beaten eggs, brandy and sugar. Beat once again. In a separate bowl, beat together the potatoes, almonds, nutmeg, lemon rind and juice. Gradually blend in the cheese mixture. Beat thoroughly. Spoon the filling into the pastry shells and bake for 35 to 40 minutes or until set. Remove from the oven and leave to cool in the tins for 10 minutes before lifting carefully on to a wire rack to finish cooling.

English Toffee Squares

English toffee is in abundance all over the country, especially in Yorkshire. These chewy toffee squares will satisfy the sweet tooth of most tea lovers.

1 cup	brown sugar, packed
2 cups	flour
pinch	salt
1 cup	butter
1	egg yolk
1 teaspoon	vanilla
6 ounces	chocolate chips
1/2 cup	chopped nuts

Preheat the oven to 350° F. Mix the sugar, flour and salt together in a large bowl. Cut in the butter. Add egg yolk and vanilla. Spread the mixture in a 15x10-inch pan and bake for 15 minutes. Melt the chocolate chips and spread over the cookie. Sprinkle with nuts and allow to cool in the pan. While still warm, cut into bars and leave in the pan until completely cold.

Sausage Rolls

These meat-filled pastries were once standard fare for most afternoon teas. A well-made meat filling is the key to a delicious sausage roll. It is worth the extra effort to make your own sausage.

1-1/4 pounds	boneless pork loin, diced
1	apple, peeled and quartered
1 cup	fresh white bread crumbs
2 teaspoons	rubbed sage
1/2 teaspoon	mace
1 teaspoon	salt
1 teaspoon	freshly ground pepper
1	egg, beaten with
1 tablespoon	heavy cream

In a food processor, blend the pork until finely ground. Add the sliced apple and continue to blend. Add the remaining ingredients and blend until well-combined. Turn out onto a floured board and divide into two 20-inch sausage rolls.

3 cups	plain flour
1 teaspoon	salt
1 cup	butter
1/2 cup	shortening
1	egg
1	egg yolk
2 tablespoons	milk
1	egg, beaten with
1 tablespoon	milk

Sift the flour and salt in a large bowl. Rub in the sliced butter and shortening until mixture has a sandy texture. In a separate bowl, whisk together the egg, egg yolk, and milk. Add this to the flour and use a fork to form a soft dough. Shape the dough into a ball, wrap in plastic and refrigerate for 1 hour.

Preheat the oven to 375° F. Cut the pastry in two. Roll half the pastry into a 20x10-inch rectangle. Cut in half lengthwise to make 2 oblongs. Place a roll of pork fillings down the middle of each oblong. Brush the edges with egg wash and fold over to enclose the filling. Press and pinch the edges together.

Cut each roll in half and place all 4 rolls on a lightly greased baking sheet. Brush with egg and slice steam vents at 1-inch intervals. Repeat with the other half of the pastry. Bake for 25 minutes. Allow to cool for 5 minutes before slicing. Serve warm. Leftover rolls may be frozen for future use.

The Original
Maids of Honour
→
MORNING
COFFEE
—
LUNCHEONS
—
CREAM TEAS

OPPOSITE
CUMBERLAND GATE
KEW GARDENS
081 940 2752

THE POLLY TEA ROOMS

26 High Street
Marlborough, Wiltshire

The ancient Roman town of Marlborough has long been a stopping point for weary travelers on the great road from London to Bath and Bristol. Legend has it that Merlin, the magician to King Arthur, is buried under a mound, located on the grounds of Marlborough College, and thus gave the town its name *Merle Barrow* or Merlin's Tomb.

The city centers around one of the widest high streets in England with many Georgian buildings and architectural styles which span over 300 years. The well-kept buildings now house antique shops, small hotels, restaurants, and gift shops.

Nearby, the intriguing six giant White Horses of Wiltshire, from the 19th and 20th centuries, are cut into the hillsides of the surrounding countryside. To the west of the village lies Avebury and the mysterious concentration of prehistoric circles and stones dating from 2500BC– older than Stonehenge, 21 miles to the south.

As you step off the busy cobblestone sidewalk through the doorway of the Polly Tea Rooms, your eyes are overwhelmed by the sight of shelf upon shelf of mouthwatering chocolates, red raspberry gateaux, walnut cakes, and meringues topped with strawberries and cream which fill the display cases at the entrance of this busy tea shop. Hand-tied bouquets of wheat and lavender hang drying from the exposed beams overhead. An eclectic collection of tea pots fills the walls behind the counter. For 50 years, passers-by have pressed their faces against the three fine bow-windows, peering past the antique crockery at the inviting display of tempting desserts set before the relaxing customers seated at tables draped with tidy floral tablecloths.

Neatly-uniformed ladies move briskly about the 25 tables taking orders and pouring pots of hot Indian, Earl Grey or Lapsang Souchong teas. Londoners, on a day trip, foreign tourists, and devoted locals make for an interesting mix of customers all drawn together for the same reasons—a moment of gentle conversation mixed with outstanding food served in a relaxing atmosphere.

Having placed their tea orders, customers gather around a tiered buffet table piled high with lovely pastries made daily in the kitchen by local pastry chefs. You have to pause several minutes before this mouthwatering display looking over the possibilities—pistachio and chocolate truffles, Linzer slices, rum truffles, lemon and red currant cheesecake, macaroons, cappuccino meringues and more. It is never an easy decision.

If you have the good fortune to visit at Christmastime, you will see the front door draped with fresh greenery tied with red bows, pine cones and giant Santa Claus cookies. At harvest time, bright orange pumpkins and golden gourds flow out of antique baskets onto the deep window sills. The Polly seems to have the right tea for all seasons.

Muesli Tea Bread

This tea recipe includes a common British breakfast cereal filled with natural ingredients. This might help you feel less guilty about eating so many sweets in the middle of the afternoon.

3-3/4 cups	whole wheat flour
16 ounces	muesli mix
4 ounces	margarine
2-1/2 teaspoons	baking powder
3	eggs
	milk to mix

Preheat the oven to 350° F. Mix the first 5 ingredients together until the mixture resembles bread crumbs. Add enough milk to barely produce a batter consistency. Place in a greased rectangular baking tin and bake for 20 to 30 minutes. Cool in the tin for 10 minutes before turning out on a rack. Slice when cooled.

Linzer Torte

The original Linzer Torte recipe came from Austria and usually includes almonds in the pastry. This English version uses hazelnuts.

2-1/2 ounces	butter
2-1/2 tablespoons	sugar
1	egg
1 teaspoon	lemon juice
2/3 cup	plain flour
pinch	baking powder
1/2 cup	finely ground hazelnuts

Cream the sugar and butter together until light and fluffy. Beat in the egg and lemon. Next add the flour, hazelnuts and baking powder to form a smooth paste. This can be done by hand. Chill for 25 minutes before rolling out the dough.

Filling

8 to 10 ounces	sponge cake
1	8-ounce jar seedless raspberry jam
pinch	cinnamon

In a food processor, blend the sponge cake until it resembles fine bread crumbs. Add the cinnamon and enough jam to form a smooth filling.

Preheat the oven to 350° F. Line a 6-inch flan tin or a springform pan with 3/4 of the pastry dough. Add the raspberry filling. Roll out the remaining dough and cut into lattice strips. Arrange the strips in a crisscross pattern on the top of the torte. Brush the exposed dough with beaten egg white. Bake for 20 to 30 minutes. Allow to cool before slicing and serving.

Hazelnut Shortbread

Shortbread, like scones, can be enhanced with the addition of fruit or nuts. Great shortbreads, like this hazelnut edition, are one of the features of the Polly Tea Rooms.

4 ounces	butter
1/3 cup	sugar
1-1/4 cups	plain flour
2 tablespoons	ground rice flour
1/4 cup	sliced hazelnuts

Preheat the oven to 350° F. Cream the butter and sugar together until fluffy and light. Sift the flour and ground rice flour together, and combine with the sugar mixture. Mix in the hazelnuts. Press the mixture into a greased cookie sheet. Prick with a fork and then bake for 20 minutes. Sprinkle lightly with sugar. Cut into squares or triangles while still warm. Allow to cool.

SHARROW BAY
COUNTRY HOUSE HOTEL

Pooley Bridge
Lake Ullswater, Cumbria

Nestled beneath the Lake District's Barton Fell, Sharrow Bay Country House Hotel—which is reputed to be the first Country House hotel to be created in Great Britain–is on the northeastern shore of Lake Ullswater, the waves actually lapping the wall of soft gray stone. Built in 1840, it has an interesting continental flavor reminiscent of a villa by the Italian Lakes.

The lakeside drive across Pooley Bridge from A592 is an interesting test of nerve for the first time visitor as you wind along the narrow, crooked country lane–often bordered by tall hedges which leave you guessing about what you might encounter around the next curve. You soon reach the well-manicured grounds of the former mansion, complete with one of the most spectacular views in all of Great Britain. Sailboats, mountains, and bright blue skies complete the idyllic setting.

Upon entering the Country House, one soon realizes the significance of the title. Here is a house with a unique unhurried atmosphere, complete with a gracious staff which knowingly attends to the guest's every need. The walls are lined with a "who's who" of famous personalities who are frequent guests of the popular establishment.

Afternoon tea has been a specialty of the hotel since Francis Coulson opened it in 1949 with his mother's time-honored recipes in hand. Today, all the baking is still done on premises. Meringues, scones, Grasmere gingerbread, Genoese cream sponges, and lemon cake are just a few of the regional specialties which await the fortunate guests.

The elegant tea service, complete with Minton china and silver trays, is as fine as you will find at any London hotel. What particularly sets Sharrow Bay apart from the average hotel tea is the marvelous setting. Tea may be taken in either the lounge with its panoramic vista of Lake Ullswater and its colorful sailboats, or the conservatory and its unhindered view of the sloping gardens and deep blue Lake District sky. Rich fabrics, beautiful antiques, and tasteful accessories surround you wherever you are. A comfortable, unhurried feeling permeates the atmosphere.

Afternoon tea is served ala carte and may consist of a selection of finger sandwiches, homemade breads, scones with preserves and cream, homemade cakes and pastries and an adequate selection of loose teas. Outside guests are welcome to join the daily afternoon affair. Be sure to ring ahead for reservations.

While you are here in this northern edge of the Lake District, take an outing to see the ancient remnants of Hadrian's Wall and the romantic ruins of Lanercost Priory which lie just an hour north, near the town of Brampton.

Cumberland Rum Nicky

The Cumberland ports of Whitehaven and Workington once were ports of entry for merchant ships coming from the West Indies. The ships were often laden with dark rum, spices and Barbados sugar. These ingredients found their way into a popular sticky sweet tart.

Shortcrust pastry

3 cups	plain flour, sifted
pinch	salt
8 ounces	butter (or 4 ounces butter and 4 ounces lard), at room temperature
3 to 4 tablespoons	cold water

Mix together the flour and salt. Cut in the butter with a fork until the mixture resembles coarse meal. Add enough water to make a stiff, yet pliable dough. Knead until smooth. Form into a ball and cover with plastic wrap. Refrigerate at least 30 minutes. Line the baking tin with the pastry. This remaining dough may be kept in the refrigerator for future use.

1	8-inch baking tin, lined with shortcrust pastry
1 pound	finely chopped dates
1/3 cup	soft brown sugar
2 tablespoons	rum
1/2 cup	water
3 ounces	unsalted butter
2 pieces	crystallized ginger, chopped
1 teaspoon	allspice

In a medium saucepan, combine the chopped dates, sugar, rum and water over a low heat for 6 to 8 minutes. Stir in the butter, finely chopped ginger, and spice. Continue to stir until a mixture is formed. Remove from heat and allow to cool.

Preheat the oven to 425° F. Pour the mixture into the prepared tin. Form a lattice work of pastry on top and bake in the middle of the oven. After 15 minutes, lower the heat to 350° F and bake for another 15 minutes or until the pastry is a light golden brown. Allow to cool and serve with whipped cream.

Grasmere Gingerbread

The Lake District village of Grasmere was home to the poet Wordsworth. He lies, with the rest of his family, in the quiet graveyard, within a stone's throw of the River Rothay. Grasmere Gingerbread is known for its potent use of ginger, both crystallized and dried. You may want to serve a dollop of cream along with this dessert.

4 ounces	butter, cold
1-1/2 cups	plain flour
1/2 teaspoon	baking soda

Mix the above ingredients together.
Combine the following ingredients in a separate bowl:

1 teaspoon	ground ginger
1/2 cup	dark soft brown sugar
1 piece	crystallized ginger, chopped
teaspoon	corn syrup

Preheat the oven to 325° F. Combine the two mixtures and mix by hand. Prepare a 6x12-inch baking tray by lining it with greaseproof paper. Spread the mixture to about 1/2-inch thickness and compress gently.

Bake for 20 minutes or until the cake begins to pull away from the sides of the pan. Allow to cool slightly and cut into squares while still warm.

Lemon Curd

This tart accompaniment to scones and cakes is most often found in Scotland and Northern England where it is sometimes referred to as lemon cheese. It is simple to make and lasts for two weeks when refrigerated.

3	eggs
1/2 cup	unsalted butter, melted
1/2 cup	fresh lemon juice
1 cup	sugar
	zest of 1 lemon

In the top part of a double broiler, beat the eggs until frothy. Stir in the lemon juice, sugar, zest, and melted butter. Place over simmering water. Stir constantly for 20 minutes. The mixture should become slightly thickened.

Remove from heat and spoon into a pint-sized container. Cool to room temperature, cover and refrigerate for at least two hours before serving. Keeps well for two weeks.

Raspberry Tarts

Tarts are always a proper tea dessert, especially when encased in a glorious spun sugar nest. This recipe for a raspberry tart is quite simple.

4 cups	all purpose flour
1/4 teaspoon	salt
2 tablespoons	sugar
1 cup	butter, sliced cold
2	egg yolks
4 teaspoons	cold water
1/2 cup	confectioners' sugar
1-1/2 cups	fresh strawberries
3/4 cup	red currant jelly

Sift together the flour and salt. Add the sugar. Cut in the butter until the mixture resembles coarse meal. In a separate bowl, combine the egg yolks and lemon juice. Add this to the flour and mix with a knife until the dough comes away cleanly from the sides of the bowl. You may add a little cold water to obtain the correct consistency. Turn out onto a lightly floured surface and knead until the dough just holds together. Wrap the dough in plastic and refrigerate at least 30 minutes.

Preheat the oven to 400° F. Grease 20 3-inch tart pans. Roll the pastry out thinly on a floured surface. Using a 4-inch cookie cutter, cut out 20 pastry rounds. Line the tins and prick the bottom of the pastry lightly with a fork. Bake for 10 minutes. Remove the pastry shells and cool on a rack. Dust the rims with confectioners' sugar and arrange the raspberries in the shells.

In a small saucepan, warm the jelly until it just melts. Use a pastry brush to glaze the fruit. Refrigerate and garnish with small pansy blooms or mint sprigs.

SHEILA'S COTTAGE

The Slack
Ambleside, Cumbria

The best of all worlds lies hidden away between England's highest mountains and its northwest sea coast. In this Cumbrian Lake District you find fairy tale fells and lakes; walking trails; character towns to explore; superb restaurants and lodgings; excursion boats and trains; ancient castles, abbeys, and stone circles; alpine-like scenery; and literary figures you have known about since childhood. This is the land of William Wordsworth and Beatrix Potter.

The village of Ambleside lies at the north end of Lake Windermere, one of the major resort lakes of northern England. You may arrive there by driving the coast from the north or south along what has to be one of the most scenic lakeside roadways in all of Britain. If you happen to be staying south in Bowness-on-Windermere, you may board the lake steamer which makes its way from Lakeside to Ableside. You get the feeling that the town is almost a part of the hills because most of the buildings, built of local stone in the traditional style which forgoes the use of mortar in the outer walls, blend into their mountain setting.

Turning under an archway off the Market Place near the post office, you walk down a narrow street known as The Slack. You immediately come to one of the area's best known eating establishments, Sheila's Cottage. This 250-year-old slate-roofed coachman's shelter has been turned into a split level restaurant with papered walls and dark pine furnishings.

The fabulous sweets, which change regularly, are a sight to behold. A seasonal specialty is a pear and ginger cake served warm with sauce Anglaise. Their Borrowdale tea bread is made with fruit steeped in tea and served with a tangy Lancashire cheese, made locally. But the dessert not to be missed is the sticky toffee pudding, so well known that *Gourmet* magazine once published their authentic recipe.

Sticky Toffee Pudding

This delightful toffee pudding can be found on the menus of many fine restaurants throughout the Lake District. The recipe is easy to make. Be sure to serve it warm out of the oven.

	unsalted butter for baking dish
1 cup and 1 tablespoon	all purpose flour
1 teaspoon	baking powder
3/4 cup	pitted dates
7 tablespoons	unsalted butter
3/4 cup	granulated sugar
1	egg, lightly beaten
1 teaspoon	baking soda
1 teaspoon	vanilla
1-1/4 cup	boiling water
5 tablespoons	packed brown sugar
2 tablespoons	heavy cream
	whipped cream for topping

Heat the oven to 350° F. Butter an 8x6-inch baking dish.

Sift the flour and baking powder onto a sheet of waxed paper or into a bowl; set aside. Chop the dates fine; toss with 1 tablespoon flour in a small bowl.

Beat 4 tablespoons of butter and 3/4 cup sugar in large bowl until mixture is light and fluffy. Beat in the egg along with a little of the flour mixture; beat for 1 minute. Beat in remaining flour mixture.

Add dates, baking soda and vanilla to the 1-1/4 cups boiling water, stirring to combine; add to batter, beating until well blended. Pour batter into a prepared baking dish; bake until set and well browned on top, 35 to 40 minutes. Remove from oven to wire rack.

Heat broiler. Heat remaining 3 tablespoons butter, the brown sugar and the 2 tablespoons heavy cream in a small heavy saucepan over medium heat to simmering; simmer until thickened, about 3 minutes. Remove from heat; pour topping over pudding. Place pudding in broiler, about 4 inches from source of heat; broil until top is bubbly, about 1 minute. Serve warm with whipped cream.

Syllabub

This drink is derived from the Old French name for champagne, "sille". The Tudors must have drunk it. What we have today is an elegant frothy affair served in its own glass. It is one of England's great treats and is brought forth for special occasions.

1	orange
4 tablespoons	confectioners' sugar
1/3 cup	Madeira
1 1/4 cups	heavy cream

Grate the rind from the orange and squeeze the juice into a cup. Combine the juice, sugar, rind, and Madeira into a bowl. Cover and allow to stand for a few hours.

Strain the liquid into a mixing bowl and stir in the cream. Beat until the mixture begins to hold its peaks. Pour into beautiful glasses (real syllabub glasses if you can find them). Serve immediately or chill overnight. Decorate with candied fruit or fresh rind if you wish.

Potted Morecambe Bay Shrimps

Morecambe Bay lies at the southern edge of the Lake District. It is famous for the tiny succulent shrimp which supply the abundance of fine restaurants found in the area. The shrimp, when potted, are often spread on toast for afternoon tea.

8 ounces	butter
1 pound	fresh shrimp, peeled
1 teaspoon	ground mace
pinch	cayenne pepper
pinch	fresh nutmeg
1/2 teaspoon	salt

Clarify the butter by melting it in a saucepan over low heat. Allow to stand at room temperature until the butter separates. Pour the butter through a cotton sieve to remove some of the fat. Reheat 3/4 of the clarified butter in a saucepan.

Add the shrimp, mace, cayenne pepper, and nutmeg. Stir over low heat until the shrimp are just cooked. Do not overcook. Add the salt to taste. Place the shrimp in small individual ramekins. Pour the remaining clarified butter over each in order to seal. Refrigerate. When set, serve with hot toast.

ST. TUDNO HOTEL

The Promenade
Llandudno, North Wales

Until the middle of the 19th century, Llandudno was a sleepy fishing village lying in the gentle curve of Conwy Bay at the top of Northern Wales. Then the railway came bringing tourists from Liverpool, Chester and the industrial cities of the Midlands. Soon a grand Victorian garden town on the sea sprang up, complete with a cupola-covered promenade, hotels, shops and amusements. On a sunny day, the Victorian houses lining the bay are still a picture of gleaming white symmetry. Visitors often refer to the well-kept resort as the "Naples of the North" so it is no surprise that this retreat has played host to such illustrious visitors as Napoleon III, Bismarck, Disraeli, Gladstone and Churchill.

It was in 1861 that the best-known Alice in all the world came to stay along the Promenade at the stylish St. Tudno Hotel. Rev. Henry George Liddell, Dean of Oxford's Christ Church, his wife, five children, footman, lady's maid, nurse, nursery maid and governess all came here on Easter holiday. This was the first of many vis-

its to Llandudno for eight-year-old Alice Pleasance Liddell. The following year, her father purchased a nearby holiday house, *Penmorfa*, which the family visited regularly until 1873.

By the time Alice was four years old, she had met Charles Lutwidge Dodgson (Lewis Carroll), a twenty-four-year-old Oxford mathematics lecturer and part-time photographer. He frequently called upon the Liddell daughters at their Oxford home to painstakingly pose the girls for a series of photographs. It was in the summer of 1862 that Dodgson picnicked with Alice and her sisters along the Thames and read to them the first of many tales later to be published as *Alice's Adventures in Wonderland*.

The award-winning St. Tudno Hotel takes its name from Llandudno's namesake who made a visit here in the sixth century. For those who, like Alice, look forward to a proper tea, this is the setting for the finest afternoon tea in all of Wales.

Afternoon tea is best enjoyed in one of the cozy front drawing rooms with their

Llandudno is an easy drive from the English towns of Chester, Liverpool or Manchester. It is ideally situated for excursions into nearby Snowdonia National Park with its rugged mountain vistas; the remote island of Anglesey; or a host of castles which seem to lie around every bend of the road. As in the Scottish Highlands, patriotic history and picturesque landscape, myth and art have combined into a romantic vision of Northern Wales. It is an area of great natural beauty too often overlooked by travelers on tight schedules.

Sweet Bara Brith

This is a traditional Welsh tea bread served with butter. The fruit may be soaked in red wine instead of tea if you wish.

2 cups	mixed dried fruit
1-1/4 cup	cold tea
1 cup	brown sugar
2-1/4 cup	self-rising flour
1	egg, beaten
1-1/2 teaspoons	allspice

In a medium bowl, combine the dried fruit, tea and sugar. Let stand un-refrigerated overnight.

Preheat oven to 325° F. Line and grease a loaf pan. Add the flour, beaten egg and allspice. Bake 1-1/2 hours or until a cake tester comes out dry from the center of the loaf. Remove to a rack and allow to cool for 15 minutes before slicing. Serve with butter or clotted cream.

cheerful bay windows looking out across the Irish Sea. Pastry chef Doris Roberts lovingly bakes all the traditional Welsh sweets which you find on the bountiful tea tray: warm, buttery Bara Brith; sweet Welsh Cakes, hot from the griddle; layered Orange Spongecake, filled with lemon curd; and warm scones accompanied by Devonshire cream and preserves. The Full Afternoon tea also includes a selection of traditional tea sandwiches—tomato, egg, cucumber or smoked salmon. The Deluxe Afternoon Tea adds strawberries with cream and a stem of champagne. A variety of fine teas from Taylors of Harrogate rounds out the fare.

With all this beautiful Welsh food, attentive service and gentle atmosphere, afternoon tea takes on a magical spell here—one even Alice would have considered a wonderland experience.

Welsh Cakes

Welsh cakes were once make in Dutch ovens placed in front of the fire in a fireplace. Today they are cooked on griddles or a heavy frying pan. This simple recipe will make 10 round cakes. They are best served warm and spread with butter.

1-1/2 cups	plain flour, sifted
1/2 cup	sugar
pinch	salt
3/4 teaspoon	ground nutmeg
1/2 cup	butter
1/2 cup	currants
1	egg, beaten
2 tablespoons	milk

Combine flour, sugar, salt and nutmeg in a bowl. Cut in the butter until the mixture sticks together. Using a fork, add currants and egg until a stiff dough is formed. Add milk only if the dough is too dry.

Roll the dough out on a floured board to a thickness of 3/4-inch. Cut out 3-inch circles using a floured cutter. Warm the griddle to medium heat and lightly grease.

Place cakes on the griddle and cook slowly—8 to 10 minutes per side. When the undersides are browned, carefully turn over with a spatula and brown the other side. Cakes are best served warm. They may be wrapped in linen until all the cakes are ready to serve. Spread lightly with butter when serving.

Orange Sponge Cake
with Lemon Curd Filling

This light Victorian cake is the type of teatime sweet which has been enjoyed for over 100 years in the seaside resort of Llandudno. The addition of a tart lemon curd filling makes it moist and delicious.

2 cups	butter, softened
2 cups	sugar
6	eggs
2	oranges, juice and zest of the rind
3 cups	plain flour
1 tablespoon	confectioners' sugar

Preheat oven to 325° F. Grease and line two 8-inch round tins. Beat together the butter and sugar until fluffy. Add eggs, orange juice, and orange zest. Beat well. Add flour and beat slowly until combined. Turn into the prepared tin and bake for 1 hour or until a skewer comes out clean. Remove from oven and allow to cool in the tin.

Make lemon curd using the recipe found on page 73.

Assemble the two cooled cakes with a lemon curd filling between the layers. Using a fine sieve, lightly dust the top with confectioners' sugar.

THE SWAN

High Street
Lavenham, Suffolk

Time seems to have stood still for over 350 years in the small Suffolk village of Lavenham. The term "dyed in the wool" originated in this medieval wool town for raw wool was once dyed in wooden vats before being woven into beautiful blue fabric here. The wool trade is long gone, but what remains are over 300 well-preserved, half-timbered buildings, sometimes sitting at gravity-defying angles, lining the narrow winding streets. They continue to serve as shops, tea rooms, and private homes in this small picture-perfect country village set amongst the rolling farmlands northeast of London.

The local skyline is dominated by the tower of Lavenham's parish church of Saint Peter and Saint Paul, soaring 141 feet into the English sky. Completed in 1515 with contributions from wealthy wool merchants, the church tower houses the beautiful Lavenham Bells, well-known in bell-ringing circles.

The story of the bells takes you to the Swan Hotel, for it was in the hotel's pub that the church bell ringers came to practice their change-ringing on a small 13-bell set of English handbells–rather than the huge tower bell–so as not to disturb the peace of the neighboring countryside. Interestingly, the bells still hang over the Swan bar. Also on display is a collection of air badges and signatures left behind by American airmen who frequented the pub while stationed nearby during World War II.

For many, the perfect English inn is synonymous with hospitality, good food and drink, open fires, and great antiquity. Visitors, treading in the footsteps of their forefathers and speculating on the happenstance of generations long gone, expect the coziness of oaken beams and the warmth of a genial host—and in The Swan, they are not disappointed. The three houses from which the hotel has developed are recorded from 1425, and the oldest part of the house bears traces of late fourteenth century workmanship. It is not known when the conversion to an inn took place, but it was well-established as such by 1667.

You may choose your table for afternoon tea at several inviting locations

throughout the rambling old-world lounge: beside a roaring fireplace, at a couch drenched in warm afternoon sun streaming in through wavy leaded-glass windows, in a secluded alcove separated from the world by ancient exposed timbers or, on a pleasant spring day, on the cloistered garden lawn surrounded by multicolored pansies, phlox, climbing wisteria, and neatly trimmed evergreens.

Afternoon tea at the Swan is a family affair presided over by Chef Andrew Barras and his wife, Anabette. Anabette bakes scones and fresh pastries every morning in the hotel's modern, well-equipped kitchen. She also makes delicious preserves weekly from whatever fruit is in abundance at the local market.

The choice of teas includes a special blend of Assam and Ceylon (described as the Queen Mum's favorite), Earl Grey, Assam, Darjeeling, or Lapsang Souchong.

Son Richard presents the tiered silver tray laden with all the expected accompaniments for the perfect full tea—egg salad on granary bread, sliced cucumbers on buttered white bread, golden brown scones set among pots of clotted cream and homemade preserves, and an assortment of spectacular pastries. These might include lemon curd tarts laced with curled lemon peels and cream, feather-light chocolate eclairs, cream tarts topped with fresh blueberries and dusted with powdered sugar, almond tarts with a flaky crust, and twin meringues with cream and chocolate shavings—all presented in elegant style.

A superb afternoon tea mystically causes you to feel good about yourself and the world in which you live. You leave your empty tea cup at the Swan with a fortunate feeling that you have participated in one of life's simple pleasures in what has to be one of England's best preserved villages.

Alternate adding the oil, flour, cinnamon, and salt. Mix well. Add the grated carrots and chopped walnuts.

Pour the batter in the 2 pans. Bake for 25 to 30 minutes. Remove from oven and allow to cool in pan.

Frosting

8 ounces	cream cheese, room temperature
2 tablespoons	milk
1 ounce	sugar
1 teaspoon	vanilla

Beat the first 4 ingredients together. Spread the frosting evenly over the cooled cakes. Sprinkle the tops with coconut. Store the cakes in a closed container in the refrigerator.

Frosted Carrot Bars

It may seem surprising that Carrot Cake is found in many tea rooms in central England. Some tea shops say it was the American soldiers stationed there during World War II who requested local bakers to recreate the traditional cakes they remembered from home. These bars are an adaptation to the familiar layered cake recipe.

4	eggs
2 cups	sugar
1/2 cup	vegetable oil
2 cups	flour
2 teaspoons	baking soda
2 teaspoons	cinnamon
1 teaspoon	salt
2 cups	grated carrots
1-1/2 cups	chopped walnuts

Preheat the oven to 350° F. Prepare two 9x13-inch baking pans.

Sift the flour with the baking soda. Set aside. Beat the eggs until light, then add the sugar.

Genoa Fruit Cake

This is the best sort of fruit cake–rich and moist but not too dark or bitter. When soaked in whiskey or rum, it will keep indefinitely.

6 ounces	butter, room temperature
1 cup	demerara sugar
	(or granulated sugar)
1/2 cup	light corn syrup
3	eggs
1 cup	currants
1 cup	sultanas (golden raisins)
1 cup	raisins
1 cup	cut mixed peel
1/4 cup	candied cherries, quartered
1/4 cup	ground almonds
1/2 cup	walnuts, chopped (optional)
1-3/4 cups	flour
1 teaspoon	baking powder
3/4 cups	milk
4 tablespoons	rum, whiskey, or brandy

Preheat the oven to 225° F. Grease and line a 9-inch round cake pan with a double thickness of greaseproof paper.

Cream the butter, sugar, and syrup together until pale and fluffy. Beat in the eggs, one at a time. Mix all the dried fruits, peel, and cherries together.

Sift the ground almonds, flour, and baking powder together. Stir the fruit into the flour, then fold in the creamed mixture, walnuts, and milk.

Pour the batter into the prepared pan and bake for 4 hours or until a skewer inserted into the center of the center of the cake comes out clean. Remove from oven and allow to cool in the pan. Wrap the cooled cake in a cheesecloth soaked with liquor. Place the cake in a closed container or wrap completely with foil. Store in a cool place for several days before slicing.

Mincemeat Pie

Mincemeat is a concoction of marmalade, apples, nuts, sugar, candied peel, raisins, spices, and suet that is minced and mixed with brandy. When made fresh and stored in airtight jars, it gets better with age. Be assured that the mincemeat served at the Swan is homemade. This recipe is an easy adaptation using a commercial mincemeat.

Pastry

3 cups	flour
pinch	salt
12 ounces	butter
2	egg yolks
4 teaspoons	sugar
	cold water

Mix together the flour and salt. Cut in the butter until the mixture resembles breadcrumbs. Make a well in the middle, add egg yolks and sugar. Mix by hand. Add enough water to give a stiff but pliable dough. Continue to knead until smooth. Wrap in plastic and chill for at least 20 minutes.

Pie filling

2	18-ounce jars of prepared mincemeat
2 tablespoons	brandy
1/4 cup	sherry
1	egg yolk
1	tablespoon cream

In a mixing bowl, combine the mincemeat, brandy, and sherry until well blended. Roll out 1/2 the sweet pastry to form a 12-inch circle. Place into a 9-inch pie pan and trim the edges. Preheat the oven to 425° F.

Spoon the mincemeat filling into the pastry shell. Roll out the remaining pastry to form a 12-inch circle. Place over the filling and make several slits to allow steam to escape. Leave a half-inch of pastry overhanging the edge. Tuck this overhang under the bottom crust and seal. Lightly brush the top (not the edge) with egg yolk beaten with cream.

Bake for 30 minutes or until the crust is golden brown. Remove to a cooling rack.

Sauce

2/3 cup	soft butter
2 tablespoons	brandy
2 cups	unsifted confectioners' sugar

In a small bowl, mix together all the ingredients. Beat at medium speed until smooth and fluffy. Store in the refrigerator. Place slices of the slightly warm pie on a dessert plate and pour the sauce over the pie. Serves 9.

THE TEA HOUSE

College Farm
Fitzalan Road, London

Within the souls of many big city residents there is a nostalgia for a return to the simple pleasures of life which seem to have disappeared amidst the tangle of busy streets, cabs, and trains which modern Londoners find themselves caught up in daily. Although London has designed some of the most beautiful parks and green spaces you will find in any world class city, there is a simple desire by London families to occasionally experience a glimpse of rural farm life, even if only for a few hours. For some, a visit to the London Zoo fills the need; for others, a trip to grandmother's farm will suffice. Many London families have discovered an easier way of finding a taste of rural life.

In the northern part of London, just off Regents Park Road near Henly's Corner, there has been a working farm since medieval times. In 1882, the founder of Express Dairy bought what was then a sheep farm and turned its 1864 barn into a tiled dairy parlor lit with skylights located in the cupola.

The amazing thing is that twentieth cen-

tury urban development has bypassed these 20 acres. By 1920, most of the surrounding farms had been sold to developers building homes for Londoners wanting to move to the suburbs. The dairy parlor was converted into a stylish tea room which soon attracted a steady clientele. Luckily, the surrounding pastures were kept intact. But, by the 1980s, quaint tea rooms were no longer in vogue and the parlor became a shabby refreshments room. The rare Blue Minton wall tiles, long-forgotten, had been covered by seven layers of wallpaper and paint. It was then that local caterer Su Russell discovered the wonderful building with its high ceiling and unique oval layout. She spent many lonely hours scraping the walls until she uncovered the treasured Blue Minton tiles.

Working from an old photograph, she restored the room to its original charm with bentwood chairs, a checkered floor, and antique tables covered with her own collection of handmade linens and fresh flowers. Friends and local antique dealers have helped her collect the lovely Willow Pattern china she now uses for her guests.

Everywhere you look you are reminded of the past. She has a colorful collection of old tea boxes and wrappers, many still holding the original contents.

Unfortunately, this teatime wonderland is open only on Sundays and bank holidays. A wide selection of teas and fresh scones with clotted cream and homemade preserves make up the limited menu.

Outside, a menagerie of animals—from pigs to peacocks–are there for your enjoyment. This farmlike setting makes a wonderful afternoon for families with children. Most of all, Su is keeping alive a fascinating piece of London history.

Shrewsbury Cakes

Many British villages have bread, buns, or cakes named after them. These simple buns are said to have come from the Trashier town of Shrewsbury– pronounced "Shrosbry."

8 ounces	butter, softened
1/2 cup	confectioners' sugar
1	egg, beaten
1 tablespoon	caraway seeds
2 cups	flour

Preheat oven to 350° F. Soften the butter and beat it with the sugar until fluffy. Add the beaten egg and caraway seeds. Stir in the flour, adding enough to make a stiff paste, and roll the dough out on a floured cloth. Cut into circles with a tumbler or cookie cutter.

Bake on a greased baking sheet for 10 minutes. Serve hot and spread with raspberry jam and cream.

Watercress Tea Sandwiches

These dainty sandwiches have been associated with British afternoon tea events for as long as anyone can remember. Luckily, these lightweights do not diminish the appetite, thereby leaving a healthy craving for the sweet tray which will pass later.

1/2 cup	butter, room temperature
1/2 cup	finely cut watercress
1 tablespoon	finely cut chives
3/4 teaspoon	Worcestershire sauce
pinch	salt
dash	pepper
1 loaf	fresh bread, sliced thin and frozen

Combine all the filling ingredients. Cut the frozen bread into crustless rounds with 2-inch round cutter. (Bread cuts more easily when frozen.) Spread the filling on half the rounds. Place the other rounds on top. Cover the sandwiches with a lightly dampened paper towel and refrigerate. Makes 36 sandwich rounds.

Almond Pudding

Bread puddings have been around for centuries. This almond flavored dessert is best enjoyed when served warm with a compote of fresh raspberries or cherries.

2 cups	milk
2/3 cup	double cream
2/3 cup	fresh white breadcrumbs
1/4 cup	sugar
1 cup	ground almonds
3	eggs, beaten
1/4 stick	butter

Preheat the oven to 300° F. Warm the milk and cream; pour over the breadcrumbs. Add the sugar and almonds and allow to soak for 10 minutes. Add the beaten eggs and stir well.

Grease a baking dish (or individual ramekins) and pour in the mixture. Dot with butter, place in a warm bath, and bake for 30 minutes. Serve with a fruit compote.

TETBURY GALLERY TEAROOM

Market Place
Tetbury, Gloucestershire

The quiet market town of Tetbury, set in the midst of the Cotswolds, was rather unknown until the 1980s when the Prince of Wales and Princess Diana chose nearby Highgrove House as their country residence. The occasional presence of royalty now draws a greater number of tourists to this "Cotswold gem"; however, the royal residence is not open to the public.

In prehistoric times Tetbury was the site of a hill fort, later taken over by the Romans. During the middle ages its prosperity grew with the establishment of a regional wool market, as evidenced by the fine merchants' houses and craftsmen's cottages that still exist throughout the town today. The Old Market House, dating from 1655, stands in the center of town and, on Wednesdays, is filled by local vendors selling antiques and general merchandise.

Legend has it that at the bottom of Gumstool Hill was a pool where scolding wives and those guilty of minor misdemeanors were tied to a ducking stool or "gumstool" and ducked under water as punishment.

Students of church architecture have known Tetbury for years for it is the site of the Parish Church of St. Mary, described by one official as "the best Georgian Gothic church ever seen." The spire is the fourth highest in England.

In the vicinity of the Old Market House, and directly across the street from the post office, stands an elegant 18th century Georgian house which now serves the dual role of tea shop and art gallery. As you enter the handsome red doorway, take a moment to browse the salon filled with English art to your right before entering the tea room. The quiet dining room holds but a few tables dressed with white linen tablecloths and set with fine bone china. Sketches, paintings, and watercolors–both old and new–cover the walls. A walled courtyard, filled with flowering plants, hosts the overflow guests on warm days.

One of the advantages of taking tea in a small tea shop includes the opportunity to get to know the owners who often function as chef, dishwasher, housekeeper, and gardener. The co-owners of the Gallery Tearoom are Jayne Maile and Helen Joyner. These genial hosts bake their cakes and scones fresh daily for their steady stream of local residents and tourists who stop in.

Among the many delicious cakes which Jane and Helen serve daily are a moist carrot cake, orange cake, chocolate coffee cake, and iced walnut cake. Beautiful food and exquisite art all served up in a fashionable setting—a perfect way to spend an afternoon.

Ladyfingers

Serve these light cakes plain or put them together in pairs with whipped cream, custard, lemon curd, or softened cream cheese blended with chopped crystallized ginger.

3	eggs, separated
1 teaspoon	vanilla
1/2 cup	superfine sugar
1 tablespoon	sugar
pinch	salt
2/3 cup	cake flour, sifted
1/2 cup	confectioners' sugar

Preheat the oven to 300° F. Beat the egg yolks, vanilla, and sugar with a large whisk until the mixture ribbons or leaves a distinct trail when whisk is drawn through the mixture.

In another bowl, beat the egg whites with salt and one tablespoon of sugar. Bring the egg whites to a peak. Mix the flour into the yolk mixture. Fold in the egg whites until the mixture is airy.

Fit a pastry bag with a plain °-inch nozzle. Pipe four-inch lengths of the mixture onto a buttered and floured baking sheet. Dust each lightly with confectioners' sugar. Brush away the excess using a dry pastry brush. Bake for 15 to 20 minutes. Remove to a wire rack to cool. Dust with the remaining confectioners' sugar.

Iced Walnut Cake

The Gallery Tea Room is known for its outstanding cakes. The butter cream filling of this cake keeps contented guests coming back again and again.

5-1/2 ounces	butter
1 cup	sugar
4	eggs, beaten
1/4 teaspoon	vanilla
4 ounces	ground almonds
1 cup	self rising flour
1 ounce	walnuts, finely chopped
4 tablespoons	milk

Grease and line a 9-inch round cake tin. Preheat oven to 300° F. Cream together the butter and sugar until light and fluffy. Gradually add eggs and vanilla, beating well to avoid curdling. Stir in ground almonds. Gently stir in flour and walnuts. Add milk to make a soft consistency.

Spoon mixture into cake tin and bake for 75 minutes until firm to the touch. Remove from tin and cool on a wire rack.

Filling

1-1/2 ounces	butter, room temperature
1-1/2 cups	confectioners' sugar
3 drops	vanilla
3 tablespoons	cream or milk

Add half the confectioners' sugar to softened butter and beat well. Beat in vanilla, remaining sugar and enough cream or milk to make a fine spreading consistency. Split cake in half, sandwich together with the filling in the middle.

Icing

3 cups	confectioners' sugar, sifted
	cold water
6	walnut halves

Mix sugar with a little water to make a thick constancy. Quickly spread over top and sides of cake using a knife dipped in cold water to smooth the surface. Leave in a cool place to set, about 2 hours. When firm to the touch, arrange walnut halves around the edge.

Banbury Cakes

"Ride a cockhorse to Banbury Cross and see fine lady upon a fine horse. With rings on her fingers and bells on her toes, she shall have music wherever she goes." As in most English market towns, there has been a cross at the intersection of the two main roads in the market square of Banbury for centuries. Banbury Cross and Banbury Cakes are what make this town famous. The bakery where Banbury cakes were first made no longer exists. Fortunately, the famous pastries live on in many parts of Britain.

Pastry

1 cup	plain flour
pinch	salt
12 ounces	butter, chilled
1 teaspoon	lemon juice
3 tablespoons	cold water

Mix together the flour and salt. Cut in small pieces of butter and blend with a pastry knife. Make a well in the middle and add the lemon juice. Mix with enough water to produce an elastic dough. On a floured board, roll out the dough to a long strip, keeping the sides straight and the corners square. Fold up the bottom third and fold down the top third.

Turn the dough so that the folded edges are to your right and left. Repeat this rolling and folding process three times, chilling the pastry for 15 minutes between the third and fourth sequence. Chill an additional 30 minutes before using.

Filling

2 ounces	butter
3/4 cup	currants
1/2 cup	mixed candied peel
1/4 teaspoon	ground cinnamon
1/2 teaspoon	allspice
1 tablespoon	light brown sugar
1 tablespoon	rum
	milk
1	egg white, beaten
	confectioners' sugar

Melt the butter in a small sauce pan and then add the dried fruit, spices, brown sugar and rum. Stir and allow to cool.

Preheat the oven to 450° F. Grease 2 baking sheets.

On a lightly floured board, roll out the pastry to 1/4-inch thickness and cut into 4-inch rounds. Place a spoonful of the fruit mixture on each round. Dampen the edges with a little milk and fold the pastry over to enclose the filling. Flatten slightly with a rolling pin and make 3 parallel slits in the top. Brush with egg white and sprinkle with confectioners' sugar. Bake for 10 to 15 minutes or until golden. Remove from the oven and allow to slightly cool on a wire rack before serving.

TIME FOR TEA

Castle Hill
Kenilworth, Warwickshire

If ever a tea room was centered around the personality of its owner—and many are—Time for Tea is the perfect example of such a match. Helena Shaw is the energetic force behind this establishment which is fast becoming the gathering place for locals and tourists in the Kenilworth area. She loves to welcome her guests into her cheerful, restored low-ceiling shop, furnished with pine tables and lined with tea pots she has collected since she was 14 years old.

Helena will gladly tell you about the resident ghost, Winnie, who has a fascination with keys and knives. As a matter of fact, a history of hauntings accompanies the entire neighboring row of quaint old shops which slowly wind up the hill outside the gate of the Kenilworth castle, begun in the 12th century by Geoffrey de Clinton. Do not miss this romantic ruin used as the setting for Sir Walter Scott's *Kenilworth*. The massive gatehouse and banquet hall have survived to this day. The village is located a few miles north of the popular medieval tourist town of Warwick, known for its great castle gloriously perched above the River Avon.

Cooking comes naturally for Helena. This young shop keeper learned the art from hours and hours spent with her 86 year-old grandmother in Yorkshire. You won't find any dainty crustless tea sandwiches here. Her hearty cheese and onion, salmon and cucumber, ham and pineapple, or cheese and chutney sandwiches are all served with crusts intact. "In Yorkshire, we don't believe in waste," she adds.

Whole wheat scones are baked daily and served with jam and cream to the delight of her devoted local guests. The selection of cakes, many from Helena's grandmother's recipes, might include chocolate and orange, date and walnut, or honey and coconut cake. Another favorite is a wonderfully moist lemon iced treacle gingerbread topped with a lemon butter icing to enhance the experience.

Helena's philosophy about her current vocation? "Tea is the punctuation mark of the day, a time when you sigh, and regain your composure." Well said and well done.

May Bolten's Date & Walnut Loaf

This is Helena's grandmother's recipe for a wonderful tea bread. This is a large recipe which makes 3 loaves. You can freeze the surplus for future use.

1/2 cup	shortening
1/2 cup	butter
2 cups	water
10 ounces	dates, chopped
5 cups	self rising flour
2 cups	sugar
2	eggs, beaten
1 cup	walnuts, chopped
1 cup	warm milk
1 teaspoon	soda

Preheat the oven to 325° F. In a saucepan, mix together shortening, butter, water, and dates. Bring to a boil, then simmer for 5 minutes. Allow to cool. Fold in flour, sugar, eggs, walnuts, and warm milk (combined with soda).

Pour mixture into 3 prepared loaf tins. Bake 1-1/2 hours at 325° F.

Lemon Iced Treacle Gingerbread

Treacle (or molasses) is a common ingredient in many British baked goods. It gives this bread a dark color and rich taste. Treacle is usually sold in tins of various sizes.

Gingerbread

1-1/3 cups	plain flour
1/2 cup	self-rising flour
1/2 teaspoon	baking soda
1 teaspoon.	ground ginger
1/2 teaspoon	ground cinnamon
1/2 teaspoon	mixed spice
1/2 cup	sugar
1	egg, lightly beaten
1/2 cup	milk
2-1/4 ounces	butter
1/2 cup	treacle or molasses

Preheat the oven to 350° F. Grease and line a 9-inch loaf pan.

Sift flours, soda, and spices into a bowl. Add sugar and combined egg and milk. Meanwhile, combine butter and molasses in a saucepan. Stir slowly until melted. Avoid boiling.

Combine dry ingredients with hot mixture. Stir well. Pour into a prepared loaf pan. Bake for 50 minutes. Turn onto wire rack and cool.

Icing

2-1/4 ounces	butter
1 teaspoon	grated lemon rind
1-1/3 cups	confectioners' sugar
2 teaspoons	lemon juice

Using an electric mixer, combine butter and lemon rind until a creamy consistency is reached. Gradually add sifted confectioners' sugar. Add lemon juice until mixture is spreadable. Spread over the top of completely cooled loaf.

Coffee, Apple and Sultana Cake
with Caramel Icing

This coffee cake serves double duty as a tea cake or breakfast sweet. The combination of apples and sultanas covered with a caramel icing is a real treat for all ages.

4 ounces	sultanas or golden raisins
1 tablespoon	dry instant coffee
3 ounces	butter or margarine
1 teaspoon	vanilla
1 cup	soft brown sugar
1	egg
2-3/4 cups	self-rising flour
1/2 teaspoon	ground cinnamon
1/2 teaspoon	baking soda
1	grated apple

Grease and line a 9x11-inch cake pan. Place sultanas, coffee and water in a saucepan and bring to a boil; stir. Remove from heat and allow to cool to room temperature.

Sift together the flour, cinnamon and soda.

Using a mixer, cream butter, vanilla and sugar in a bowl until light and fluffy. Beat in egg until combined.

Preheat the oven to 350° F. Transfer the mixture into a large mixing bowl and stir in half the sifted flour, cinnamon and soda. Next, add half the cooled sultana mixture. Stir in the remaining flour and then add the rest of the sultana mixture. Add remaining ingredients.

Pour the batter into the prepared cake pan. Bake for 30 minutes. Remove to a cake rack and allow to cool.

Icing

2 tablespoons	soft brown sugar
1 ounce	butter
1 tablespoon	milk
1 cup	confectioners' sugar
3 ounces	chopped walnuts

Combine the first 3 ingredients over very low heat until butter is just melted. Slowly, whisk in the confectioners' sugar. Remove from heat.

Spoon the icing over the cooled cake and top with chopped walnuts.

Ginger, Fig and Walnut Loaf

This rich tea bread is made extra moist with the addition of sour cream and figs.

6-1/2 ounces	butter or margarine
2/3 cup	sugar
3	eggs
4 ounces	figs, chopped fine
4 pieces	crystallized ginger, chopped fine
1 cup	chopped walnuts
1 cup	all purpose flour, sifted
1 cup	self-rising flour, sifted
1/3 cup	sour cream

Preheat the oven to 325° F. Grease and line a 9-inch loaf pan.

Cream butter and sugar in a small bowl with an electric mixer until light and fluffy. Beat in the eggs, 1 at a time, until well-combined. Transfer the mixture into a large bowl.

Stir in the ginger, figs and walnuts. Add the sifted flours and sour cream. Pour the batter into the prepared pan. Bake for 1-1/4 hours. Allow to stand for 5 minutes before turning out onto a wire rack to cool. Slice and serve warm or at room temperature.

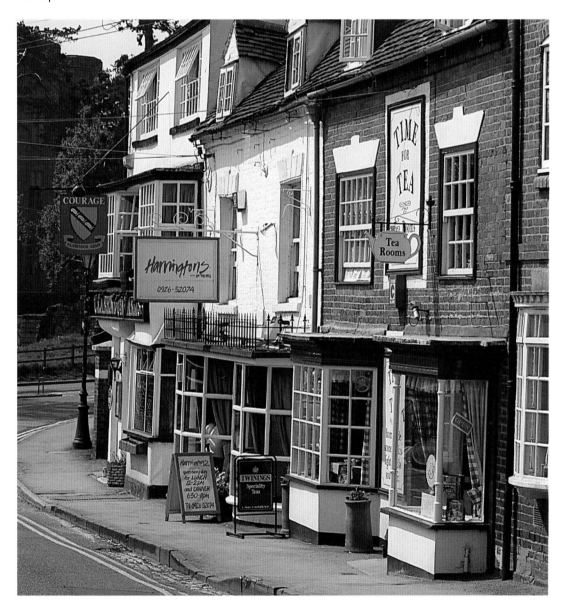

THE WALDORF PALM COURT

**Aldwych
London**

Tea and dancing were as synonymous as clotted cream and preserves when the tango was at its height of popularity around 1920. Hemlines were on the way up and tea dances were acceptable occasions where you could get physical with your favorite girl in the middle of the afternoon.

The Dancing Times wrote in May of 1913, "Whilst the Tango has carried all before it in the ballrooms of society, the afternoon salons have adopted as their own a charming little innovation from Morocco. This is the *thé-dansant* or tea dance, which is quite the latest feature of the Paris drawing rooms. Among society ladies in Morocco the custom holds that when calls are made, the hostess entertains her visitors to coffee, whilst maidens attached to the house dance for the visitors' pleasure. Very often the hostess herself dances to amuse her guests. French officials' families in Morocco and officers on the warships stationed off the coast of the new protectorate, struck with the novelty of the idea, adopted it; and at afternoon tea a gentle valse around the tea-table became a recognized fashion."

The tea dance soon spread from Paris to London where the newly-built Waldorf Hotel began hosting Tango Club afternoon teas in its grand Edwardian surroundings. The Waldorf continued hosting tea dances until World War II when a shortage of men finally brought an end to the delightful entertainment.

By 1982, a renewed interest in afternoon tea was sweeping the country and the almost forgotten tea dance was resurrected on the spacious marble floor of the Waldorf's Palm Court. A small combo accompanies the Saturday and Sunday afternoon soirees where couples of all ages may be found fox-trotting and waltzing their cares away. Middle age husbands and wives from various countries, young couples trying out their freshly-honed dance steps, senior citizens reliving a bygone era, and even mothers and sons fill the dance floor these days.

Seating may be taken at either the balcony level, where you may safely peer approvingly over the ornate wrought-iron railing covered with fairy lights, or at linen-covered tables on the dance floor where, sooner or later, the romantic mood and the rhythmic music will seduce the most reticent of tea dance voyeurs to join in the frolicsome ritual.

If chocolate is more enticing than dancing, the Friday afternoon chocolate buffet may be your "cup of tea." The creative chefs at The Waldorf showcase unbelievable sculptures, cakes, tortes, truffles, pastries and strawberries fashioned from or covered with chocolate. All this chocolate decadence is paired with a selection of teas especially chosen to compliment the occasion. This is in addition to the elegant silver tea tray laden with sandwiches of smoked salmon, egg mayonnaise and sliced cucumber. Golden scones with real Devonshire cream and preserves make up the second course. Beauti-

ful fruit-filled pastries and sweets top off the afternoon's bounty.

You can be sure that your afternoon at The Waldorf will be a unique experience in all the world. This civilized celebration from forgotten years is a glimpse of a cultural event which too soon disappeared from society's scene. The tea dance is an opportunity for travelers to take home a memory which will be shared with friends for years to come.

Brandy Snaps

Have your wooden spoon handy when these snaps come out of the oven. You will need to give them a twist while they are still warm and pliable.

1/2 cup	butter
1/2 cup	sugar
1/2 cup	syrup
2/3 cup	all purpose flour
1/2 teaspoon	allspice
1/2 teaspoon	ginger
	whipped cream

Preheat the oven to 350° F. Line 2 baking sheets with parchment paper.

Slowly heat the butter, sugar and syrup in a saucepan until melted. Remove from heat. Sift the flour, spice and ginger together. Add to the butter mixture. Mix well and drop by spoonfuls onto the parchment. Allow space for the mixture to spread.

Bake for 7 to 10 minutes or until golden brown. Remove from oven and immediately rill each snap around a greased wooden spoon handle. Allow to cool on a wire rack. Fill with whipped cream. Makes 25 snaps.

Smoked Salmon Tea Sandwiches

Smoked salmon is a regular feature at many fine hotel teas. This delicious recipe uses both a slice of smoked salmon and a salmon spread.

4 ounces	smoked salmon pieces
1-1/3 cup	heavy cream
2 tablespoons	Bourbon
1/2 teaspoon	white pepper
	whole grain bread, sliced thin
	butter, room temperature
2 ounces	smoked salmon, wafer thin

In a food processor, chop the smoked salmon until fine. Add half the cream. Remove the mixture and press through a strainer to remove liquid. Beat in the Bourbon and pepper.

Lightly butter one side of the bread slices and spread the mixture on half the slices. Place the sliced salmon on top of the mixture. Season lightly with pepper and cover with the remaining buttered bread slices. Trim the crusts and cut sandwiches in half. Keep covered with a damp cloth until ready to serve. Garnish with fresh parsley or lemon.

Strawberry Tarts

These elegant custard-filled desserts are found on many hotel tea trays. This recipe uses homemade pastry crusts. Ready made pastry shells are now available in many groceries.

Pastry

1/4 cup	flour
pinch	salt
1/4 cup	superfine sugar
4 tablespoons	butter
2	egg yolks

Sift flour and salt together. Make a well in the center and add sugar, butter and egg yolks. Work together with your hands. A few drops of water may be needed to bind the mixture together. Knead until smooth, then wrap in plastic and refrigerate for 1 hour.

Preheat oven to 375° F. Grease 8 tart tins. Roll out the pastry shell very thinly and cut into 8 circles. Press the pastry into each tin and bake for 15 to 20 minutes until golden.

Custard

1/8 cup	cornstarch
1-1/4 cup	milk
1/4 cup	sugar
2	egg yolks, beaten
6 drops	almond extract

In a saucepan, dissolve the cornstarch in a little milk. Gradually add the remaining milk, sugar and egg yolks. Bring slowly to a boil while stirring. Allow to thicken and remove from heat. Add almond flavoring; stir thoroughly. Sprinkle a tablespoon of sugar over the surface and allow to cool without stirring. When cold, beat and spoon into tart shells.

Topping

40	fresh ripe strawberries, caps removed
5 tablespoons	red currant jelly
1-1/2 tablespoons	water

Arrange the strawberries, pointed end up, over the custard. In a saucepan, heat the red currant jelly with the water to make a glaze. Bring to a boil, strain and reheat. Brush the strawberries with the glaze. Allow to set before serving.

THE WILLOW TEAROOM

Sauchiehall
Glasgow, Scotland

Guests are attracted to tea rooms for a myriad of reasons—sometimes for the food or a signature recipe, sometimes for the company of a congenial host, or sometimes for the setting. In Glasgow, you visit the Willow Tearoom because of the building's architect, Charles Rennie Mackintosh.

At the beginning of the twentieth century, businesswoman Kate Cranston employed the young artist/architect to design and decorate the interiors of her popular tea rooms located on Argyle, Buchanan, Ingram and Sauchiehall Streets. Kate was known for her flamboyant hats and Victorian dress but her art nouveau tea rooms were considered to be the latest fashion for Glasgow society. No one was more suited to set the pace for a new era than the forward thinking Rennie Mackintosh.

In the same manner of America's Frank Lloyd Wright, Mackintosh designed not only the building, but also the windows, lights, furniture, wall coverings and floors. "It is the room as a whole with which serious art should be concerned," wrote a German art critic after viewing Mackintosh's

work in 1902. The Cranston tea rooms and the unique Mackintosh style became so popular in Glasgow that the artist felt he could not leave his hometown if he wanted to make a living.

But the boom soon faded when, in 1909, he finished his last major commission, the Glasgow School of Art. Mrs. Cranston later retired from the tearoom business and his benefactors were few as the classical movement became fashionable once again. The once celebrated artist lived his final days in near poverty supporting himself by selling floral watercolors. He died, almost forgotten, in London in 1928 at the age of 60, leaving an estate valued at less than $200.

The world is fortunate to have one Mackintosh tearoom still carrying out its intended function. The Willow Tea Room sits today above a jeweler's shop on Glasgow's bustling shopping street of Sauchiehall, just as it did 100 years ago when Kate Cranston commissioned Charles Rennie Mackintosh to design it. The plain facade, art nouveau windows and definitive signage immediately let you know that this is the scheme of an out-of-the-ordinary designer.

Entrance to the tea room is through the jeweler's shop, past irresistible Mackintosh-inspired jewelry and up a flight of stairs to a mezzanine where diners once enjoyed a teatime respite. One more flight of steps leads you to the Room de Luxe, restored in 1980 to its 1903 appearance. Tea customers are often queued along these stairs waiting their turn at one of the 12 tables.

The distinctive tall back chairs, barrel ceiling and leaded glass windows immediately catch your attention. The furnishings are all Mackintosh reproductions. A large pastry display case fills the entrance, and today's guests are often dressed more casually than they were a century ago, but the signature stylings are a feast for the eyes of any Mackintosh aficionado.

Afternoon tea includes a selection of sandwiches: smoked salmon, cucumber or roast beef. Scones with butter, jam, and clotted cream are also offered. Delicious pastries, including an apple tart, sit tempting you from the dessert trolley.

Dundee Cake

The cold North Sea wind blows for much of the year into the eastern city of Dundee. The residents often brace themselves for the harsh winter weather with a cup of strong hot tea and a slice of marmalade-flavored Dundee Cake.

2 cups	all-purpose flour
1-° teaspoons	baking powder
3/4 cup	butter, room temperature
3/4 cup	sugar
3	eggs, room temperature
1/2	cup orange marmalade
16 ounces	mixed candied fruits
1cup	golden raisins
1/4 cup	orange juice flavored with brandy
1/2 cup	blanched almonds
1	egg white, slightly beaten

Preheat oven to 300° F. Grease a 2-inch deep 8-inch cake pan and line it with waxed paper. Sift together flour and baking powder into a medium size bowl. Cream the butter and sugar in a large bowl until light and fluffy. Add eggs, one at a time, then marmalade.

Gently fold in flour mixture. Stir in dried fruits and orange juice, mixing well. Pour into cake pan. Arrange almonds in a circular pattern around the top. Brush with egg white. Bake at 300° F for 1-1/2 hours or until an inserted toothpick comes out clean. Cool in pan for about one hour. Turn onto a wire rack. Serves 12.

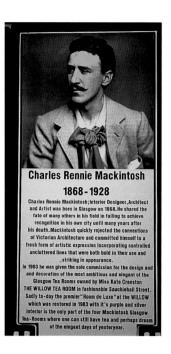

Charles Rennie Mackintosh
1868 - 1928

Charles Rennie Mackintosh; Interior Designer, Architect and Artist was born in Glasgow on 1868. He shared the fate of many others in his field in failing to achieve recognition in his own city until many years after his death. Mackintosh quickly rejected the conventions of Victorian Architecture and committed himself to a fresh form of artistic expression incorporating controlled uncluttered lines that were both bold in their use and striking in appearance.

In 1903 he was given the sole commission for the design and and decoration of the most ambitious and elegant of the Glasgow Tea Rooms owned by Miss Kate Cranston THE WILLOW TEA ROOM in fashionable Sauchiehall Street. Sadly to-day the premier "Room de Luxe" at the WILLOW which was restored in 1983 with it's purple and silver interior is the only part of the four Mackintosh Glasgow Tea-Rooms where one can still have tea and perhaps dream of the elegant days of yesteryear.

Carrot Cake Squares

This moist carrot cake is flavored with ginger. Cut into small squares, it is a sweet finale to any afternoon tea.

1-1/4 cups	canola oil
1-1/4 cups	sugar
2	large eggs
1-1/4 cups	all purpose flour
2 teaspoons	ground ginger
1 teaspoon	baking soda
1 teaspoon	baking powder
1 teaspoon	cinnamon
1/2 teaspoon	salt
2 cups	grated carrots

Preheat oven to 350° F. Line a 14-inch baking pan with parchment. Combine the oil and sugar. Whisk in the eggs, one by one. Sift in the dry ingredients and then stir in the carrots. Mix well. Pour into the prepared pan and bake for 30 to 35 minutes. Allow to cool before icing.

Icing

6 ounces	butter, room temperature
3/4 cup	cream cheese
2 cups	confectioners' sugar
1/2 teaspoon	vanilla
	crystallized ginger

Beat the butter and cream cheese until softened. Beat in sugar and vanilla. Spread the icing over the cool cake. Decorate with crystallized ginger. Cut into squares. Keeps well in a refrigerated container. Serves 18 to 20.

Bishop's Cake

Various recipes for this moist pound cake are abundant. Tradition has it that British bakers brought out their best ingredients when the Bishop came to their village.

3	eggs
1 cup	sugar
1-1/2 cups	all purpose flour
1/4 teaspoon	salt
1 teaspoon	baking powder
6 ounces	chocolate chips
2 cups	chopped walnuts
1 cup	pitted dates, chopped
1 cup	candied cherry halves

Preheat oven to 325° F. Grease and line a loaf pan. Beat the eggs and sugar together until thick. Place the fruit, nuts and chips into a large bowl. Sift the flour, baking powder and salt over the mixture. Mix well. Add the egg mixture and mix again. Pour into prepared pan. Bake for 1-1/4 to 1-1/2 hours or until a cake tester comes out clean. Remove from oven and allow to cool–in pan–on a rack. When cool, slice and serve. Serves 10 to 12.

THE GREAT TEA ROOMS OF BRITAIN

Bensons of Statford-upon-Avon
4 Bard's Walk
Stratford-upon-Avon, Warwickshire
CU37 6EY
01789 26116

Bettys Cafe Tea Rooms
1 Parliament Steet
Harrogate, North Yorkshire HG1 2QU
01423 502746

Bettys Cafe Tea Rooms
32 The Grove
Ilkley, West Yorkshire LS29 9EE
01943 608029

Bettys Cafe Tea Rooms
188 High Street
Northallerton, North Yorkshire DL7 8LF
01609 775154

Bettys Cafe Tea Rooms
6 St Helen's Square
York, North Yorkshire YO1 2QP
01904 659142

Browns
Albemarle and Dover Streets
London W1A 4SW
0171 493 6020

Bridge Tea Rooms
24A Bridge St.
Bradford-on-Avon, Wiltshire BA15 1BY
01225 865537

Canal Tea Gardens
Canal Hill
Tiverton, Devon EX16 4AQ
0884 252291

Forbes Brasserie at the Cotswold House
The Square
Chipping Campden, Gloucestershire
GL55 6AN
01386 840330

Kind Kyttock's Kitchen
Cross Wynd
Falkland, Fife, Scotland KY7 7BE
01337 857477

Le Meridien Picadilly
The Oak Room Tea Lounge
21 Piccadilly
London W1V 0BH
0171 734 8000

The Original Maids of Honour
288 Kew Road
Kew Gardens, Surrey TW9 3DU
0181 940 2752

The Polly Tea Rooms
26 High Street
Marlborough, Wiltshire   SN8 1LW
0167 251 2146

The Pump Room
Stall Street
Bath, Avon BA1 1LZ
01225 444477

The Dorchester
The Promenade
Park Lane
London   W1A 2HJ
0171 629 8888

Sharrow Bay Country House Hotel
Lake Ullswater
Howton, Cumbria CA102LZ
017684 86301

Sheila's Cottage
The Slack
Ambleside, Cumbria LA229DQ
015394 33079

St. Tudno Hotel
North Parad Promenade
Llandudno, Wales LL30 2LP
01492 874411

Swan
HighStreet
Lavenham, Sudbury CO109QA
0178247477

Taylors in Stonegate
46 Stonegate
York, North Yorkshire YO1 2AS
01904 622865

Tea House at College Farm
45 Fitzalan Road
London N3 3PG
0171 240 9571

Tetbury Gallery TeaRoom
18 Market Place
Tetbury, Glouchestershire GL8 8DD
01666 503412

Time for Tea
40 Castle Hill
Kenilworth, Warwickshire CV8 1NB
01926 512675

The Waldorf
Aldwych
London WC2B 4DD
0171 836 2400

The Willow Tearoom
217 Sauchiehall Street
Glasgow, Scotland G23EX
0141 332 0521

RECIPE INDEX